Fearsome Edifice:

A History of the Decorated *Domus* in Catholic Churches

by Dennis McNally SJ

I dedicate this book to my brother, Brian Patrick McNally,
and his family.

Brian is an architect with the firm of Pei Cobb Freed & Partners.
He has helped and inspired me all my adult life with his acuity
in viewing the works of the past,
and his drive to understand the works of the present.

Fearsome Edifice:

A History of the Decorated *Domus* in Catholic Churches

ISBN: 1-55605-348-7

Library of Congress Control Number: 2002108833

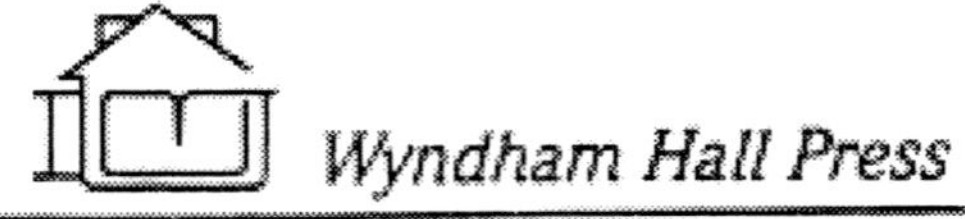

Lima, Ohio 45806
www.wyndhamhallpress.com

PRINTED IN THE UNITED STATES

Table of Contents

Presuppositions

1. All religions are looking for encounter with the "Totally Other," the "mysterium tremendum et fascinans." (Rudolph Otto)

2. The mysterium encounters the people in distinct memorable moments which are isolated in history and recalled ritually. The events happened "once upon a time," "in illo tempore." (Mircea Eliade)

3. In the Catholic tradition "illud tempus," the primordial time of the encounter with God, is focused on the life of Christ. The salvific moments of His life are ritually re-enacted, "re-presented" in such a way that the "unbloody sacrifice" of the Eucharistic Liturgy, "the 'mass'," is the most holy encounter, in time and space, with the timeless God who is Jesus, from His dimension, as it were, into ours. (Dom Odo Casel)

4. There are attitudes toward church which affect the mindset of civilizations. For the Catholic Church, five mindsets can be found in the names given for significant structural traditions:
   a. the church, "kyriake"
   b. the basilica, "basilica"
   c. the cathedral, "cathedra"
   d. the ecclesia, (église, iglesia, chiesa)"ekklesia," or the nave, "navis"
   e. the house of God, "domus" (der Dom, le dôme, il duomo, el domo)

1. These names belie (respectively) five attitudes toward Church which Avery Dulles has called the "Models of the Church":
   a. sacrifice
   b. kerygma
   c. hierarchy
   d. service
   e. mystical communion

1. The five names (also respectively) refer to the five furnishings necessary for the modern liturgy (McNally, <u>Sacred Space: an Aesthetic for the Liturgical Environment</u>, Wyndham Hall 1985):

a. the altar is the Lord's (kyriake) place of sacrifice
b. the ambo, pulpit, is the "basilican" place of the Good News, kerygma
c. the seat of the priest represents the apostolic continuity of hierarchy
d. the nave is the place of the congregation who serve one another.
e. the domus, the house of God, represents the communion of the People of God, ministers and congregation, with God within the confines of SPACE created for this mystical communion.

7. There are archetypal materials and images used in ritual architecture almost universally: (Mircea Eliade)
    a. stone
    b. tree
    c. the cosmic pillar
    d. earth
    e. sky
    f. water
    g. the mountain-city-temple (progressive entry), the cosmic center

7. There are atmospheric constants found in the ritual spaces of all identifiable religious traditions: (Gerardus van der Leeuw)
    a. silence
    b. darkness
    c. emptiness
    d. monumentality
    e. profusion

In this book we are going to "visit" a number of important sites of the history of Roman Catholic liturgy. We will consider the historical context for the structure and the adaptability of the decorated domus to the liturgy of today. For each we will consider:

I. Liturgical Appropriateness,
II. Aesthetic Appropriateness,
III. Presence of Atmospheric Descriptors, and
IV. Presence of Archetypes of Mysterium

Chapter One: The Initial Proposition

If we visit a number of historical places, considering their foundational situation and then considering their appropriateness for our present day liturgy, we might get a sense of whence we come and whither we go in liturgical-space-making. We might have a handle on our building of churches. Knowing whence we come can help us prevent doom. (Those who do not consider history are doomed to repeat it.)

The real question underneath all our visits and considerations will be, of course, whether we make space for God in our lives. Do the churches, in fact, make a place where we find it easier to encounter divinity among us?

So, let us look at some buildings keeping in mind that Art History has given us broad impressions of types of church architecture wherein thousands of buildings spanning hundreds of years and covering millions of miles get assigned to one or another historical category, one stylistic filum. We can speak of a baroque, a byzantine, or a beaux arts neo-classical building and have a very clear idea of some of its artistic characteristics.

We can also talk of the history of the liturgy and of how a building comes out of a particular historical context and continues to form the mindset of the population of that historical context. There is a neat and noticeable convergence of art and liturgical history. However, there is a way that the timeless liturgy should be able to fit into any building as the backdrop for the sacred space created in it, for and by the people who are commemorating the "sacred time," the "eternal moment," "illud tempus," of Christ's divinely continuing life. This means that there should be something timeless in the temporal world.

Illud Tempus in Our Own Time

Somehow a holy place should affect us for the sacred events that are regularly commemorated within its walls. A church is not just, therefore, a backdrop, but also a timely expression of a timeless reality. In awesome fact, churches help God become most time-bound for us and with us, whenever we celebrate a Mass. God is "helped" precisely because <u>we</u> are helped to perceive the Presence.

During the time of the living memory of the presence of Jesus, there were people for whom the memories were visceral. People knew what happened; they kept the story alive by telling stories. Time was still theirs and His. They thought the end of time was coming soon.

When that end didn't happen, the early Christians had to accommodate time's passage because of the possibility that memory of Jesus could be lost. They told the stories in a more permanent way. "In illo tempore…." At that time, or once upon a time, this happened to Jesus….. Mircea Eliade (Patterns in Comparative Religion, trans. Rosemary Sheed, New American Library, 1974, pg. 30) speaks of the primordial "kratophany" or "hierophany" as that time when a religious people has its memorable encounter with the Wholly Other, the "mysterium tremendum" which both draws and repels us. Rudoplh Otto (The Idea of the Holy, trans. John W. Harvey, Oxford University Press, 1958, pg. 12) described the mystery in ways that make the Judeo-Christian experience very much like the ones which Eliade finds all over the world at all times in history. For Otto the mystery we encounter is in "theophany," not power or holiness being revealed, but God's self-revelation and communication. Otto calls it the "unnamed something" or the "numinous" (ibid. pg. 6). In the reflection of the theological giants of that first hundred years after Jesus' death and resurrection, the primordial, pristine, and principal theophany is Jesus. The stories were about how God reached us in Jesus' words and actions. He becomes numinous so shortly after His death and resurrection.

The commemorative action which became the Mass was essentially telling the story and sharing the commemorative meal which Jesus enjoined on His disciples at the Last Supper. Josef Jungmann (The Mass: An Historical, Theological, and Pastoral Survey, trans. Julian Fernandes, S.J, ed. Mary Ellen Evans, The Liturgical Press, 1976, pg 116) tells us that there was no need for anything except telling the story and preparing, offering, and sharing the meal. The environment was inconsequential until the eternal time became something beyond living memory. In fact, he tells us that the only thing necessary was a table on which to place the bread and wine. (Public Worship, trans. Clifford Howell, S.C., The Liturgical Press, 1957, pg. 60) Then the environment became not only a space created by active memory and prayer but a place demanded by social interaction.

Gerardus van der Leeuw tells us that God has no need of a house but we need Him to need a place like our own (Sacred and Profane Beauty: The Holy in Art, trans. David E. Green, Holt Rinehart & Winston, 1963, pg. 204). This means that the space created by the commemorative words and action began to need a permanence, a signal on the human landscape that "illud tempus" is made present, with regularity, among us. God then had a tent among the people, a post-Hebraic arc of the covenant; Christ had a temple, a synagogue, in the Christian world. It soon became imperial in its accoutrements because of the course of human history within the political expediencies of powerful people like the Emperor Constantine. God then had a basilica.

So, there were upper rooms, like the original place of the Last Supper, and probably lower rooms, fields, and beachfronts in the earliest living memory of the Church. Decoration was probably event specific, if there were any decoration at all. When the space began to need its own place, the history of church architecture began, and the development of a specifically Christian religious art was initiated. The continuation of the theophany meant a sharing of holiness. The story of holiness self-manifesting is the story of the ongoing life of grace within us. The work of the Holy Spirit puts holiness into the stories of "saints," the holy ones. Some of their stories, like Jesus' own, include manifestations of wholly other worldly power. They are our "kratophanies." Thus, we soon have churches with story-telling decoration, the stories told according to doctrinal decisions worked out in patristic dialogue, conciliar documents, and papal decisions following on scriptural canonicity. The "deposit of faith" is what ecclesial decoration illustrates.

Contrary to the idea that the Eucharist can be prayed in any place, at any time is the idea that the Eucharist is going on at all times and in all places because it is Jesus who presides. It is the eternal high priest of the Epistle to the Hebrews who performs the timeless miracle. It is the Christ who is with us whenever two or more are gathered in His name. In Eliade's immortal understanding, Christ's timelessness enters into our timed existence. The infinite comes into our finite places and within the space that is created, His Holy Spirit meets ours. If our church buildings are doing their job, they will help us to focus on this PRESENCE.

Let us now look at the history of the church-as-building to see if and how this has been done, if and how it can be done. It is important to note that some fear that, if this phenomenon, the decoration of the domus, were understood well enough, it could become a cultural manipulation. In other words, some fear that such buildings do not "focus on the Presence" but they invent it! A leitmotif of our examination of this history might shed some light on the possibility or impossibility of such manipulation of the mind of mankind.

Chapter Two: Early Christian Churches

The Catacomb and the Tomb

Jungmann (Public Worship , pg. 60) tells us that the first century Christians had no churches to speak of. They used upper rooms, burial places, people's houses for the agape meal. It seems that originally the ritual reenactment was more like a Hebrew seder, served within the home, commemorating the continuation of the pilgrimage begun in the Exodus.

The need for more permanent place arose with time and distance from the actual living memory of the Christ-life. The places that we will look at first are among the earliest places that were used as those more permanent churches. The Catacomb of Priscilla was not always a place where Christians ran to hide from the evil emperor. There were many years that Christians, living in peace within the empire, buried their dead and, like their peers, both Hebrew and pagan, they would visit the dead. The ritual prayer of the Mass was early codified and the catacomb would be a natural place to pray in this ritual way, commemorating the death and resurrection of both the Lord and of the more personal bereavements of those congregating among the tombs. The excavations below St. Peter's Basilica reveal tombs like St. Peter's where the Jewish Christians of Rome would congregate even before Constantine.

The Tomb of Gala Placidia, daughter and sister to emperors of the Eastern Roman Empire, is a very small cruciform chapel that seems by its decoration to have been used for liturgy. So, it may be an early place specifically used for liturgy but not in someone's home. In Ravenna, a place soon abandoned as an imperial world crossroads, it is relatively pristine and gives us an untouched image of a really early "church."

A Little Background

The earliest liturgies of the Roman Church were commemorative events in which the successors of the apostles presided over the breaking of the bread and the passing of the wine. There was little ceremony except some singing and some praying. The different episcopal cities began to develop customs, places of more dense populations where there were concentrations of Christians, the episcopal cities, chose episcopoi, overseers, bishops. We think of them as successors to "the twelve" or the apostles. It was especially during the liturgy that the position of bishop would be seen as important. In the beginning the bishops were not a class apart. Everyman-men, they were the successors to the apostles whose authority was won within a living local community. These cities were, more than likely, where the apostles' disciples had settled. Antioch, Alexandria, Ephesus, Jerusalem, Rome, and later Constantinople, these fabled imperial places were centers of political and intellectual life. They became the seats of the bishops. Every one of them developed a liturgical tradition which was eventually "canonized," or regularized. There are precious few places left from the pre-Constantinian period when the Church was legitimized.

The Catacomb of Priscilla

Walter Lowrie in Monuments of the Early Church: A Handbook of Christian Archaeology (MacMillan 1923) says that people came here to celebrate the Eucharist in the presence of the dead, a communion of the living with the dead. Lowrie and Jungmann imply that the normal celebration of an agape, a "love-feast," would take place in an upper room, or back room, of someone's house. The room would often enough be set aside for this purpose, away from the street's noises. Jungmann describes just such a room in Missarum Solemnia (The Mass of the Roman Rite: Its Origin and Development, trans F. K. Bruner, CSSP, Vol I, pg 22, Benziger Brothers, 1955) but there are no such places around for our scrutiny.

The catacomb is described by Lowrie this way:

> Other crypts, though used likewise for burial, seem to have been designed especially for the celebration of Christian worship—particularly, one must suppose, of the eucharist. Notwithstanding their limited size, they are rightly regarded as subterranean chapels intended for a more or less public use. They open generally with a broad entrance upon the corridor, so that a number of worshippers might have been accommodated in the latter. The accommodation was sometimes still further increased by a second chapel opening directly opposite the principal one; it is supposed that this was occupied by the women. (Lowrie pg. 26)

According to Jungmann, the agape first celebrated in these places was not the Eucharist, but a sharing of bread and wine. He speaks of the early development of the Liturgy and how it came to pass that the ritual was separated from the meal:

> ...what had to be repeated as the Lord's Institution was not the meal but what in its original form has been called by Dom Gregory Dix (in The Shape of the Liturgy) a "seven-action" schema: (1) the Lord took bread; (2) gave thanks; (3) broke it; (4) distributed it with the corresponding words; (5) took the chalice; (6) gave thanks; (7) handed it to his disciples. A first step toward the adaptation to circumstances was to merge the two parts of the double action. The account of the Institution in Mark/Matthew seems to have had this liturgical practice in view.
>
> The effect was a four-action shape: (1) preparing bread and wine; (2) the thanksgiving prayer; (3) the breaking of bread; (4) the communion (pp. 48-50; 78-82). In this formula one may recognize already the "shape" of the structure of the Mass that has since come into common use, Once the two parts were thus conjoined, the meal began to be dissociated from the Eucharistic action, and the Eucharistic ritual could be performed before or after the meal. The next logical step was that this action could also take place by itself, independent of the meal. The exact date of this second step was probably contingent upon local traditions in different places. By the second century, at any rate, it is a fait accompli. (The Mass: An Historical, Theological, and Pastoral Survey, trans. Julian Fernandes, SJ, Liturgical Press, 1976. Pp. 20,21)

That this is speculative conjecture is quite evident from the use Jungmann makes of subjunctives and conditionals in this passage. There are, however, other possibilities for such speculation. Lowrie suggests, for instance, that the meal was separated from the Eucharist under the directive of St. Paul. In any case, the catacomb must be considered a liturgical space.

Now entered through a convent courtyard, the Catacomb of Priscilla had been entered though the villa of a wealthy Roman Christian. A nun typically leads the modern pilgrim down dark, narrow, stone corridors and steep stairwells. The way would have been very dark and lighted only by torch or lamplight. Passing banks of tombs, now mostly empty, laid out like bookshelves in the crowded stacks of a venerable old library. Horizontally shelved body places line the walls in soft crumbling stone.

After what seems an eternity to today's impatient tourist/pilgrim, a "large, open space" is entered. Ten or twelve feet square, the room has a stone seat at one wall, its orientation unknown at this depth beneath the serpentine descent. The visitors have entered from the left of the seat and opposite their entrance is a small room beyond. To the right is the continuation of apparently endless corridors. This space fits Lowrie's description of one originally intended for the Liturgy. The congregation would be very small.

With Lowrie's archaeology behind him the modern pilgrim can imagine the Liturgy of this earliest of Christian sacred spaces. The ancient congregation having made a similar descent would come to this room where the newly deceased might be laid in the adjacent room under the mural of the Good Shepherd or the Mother of God. The flickering light of torch or candles playing shadows on the rounded ceiling and soft stone walls and the sound of praying or singing filling the small chamber, the bishop or other officiant would intone prayer or comment on the Scripture from his throne. He would stand at the table brought along for the occasion of this Mass. The attention of the small community is necessarily riveted on the altar at the center of this small space.

The place has a mountain of historical charm, although a liturgy today might seem quite inappropriate down there. It is, after all, an archaeological dig. But the sense of what would be appropriate in those early days, before the codification of the rites, can afford a kind of pristine idea of what they thought necessary.

In the checklist approach which we developed in a previous book, Sacred Space, we find that there are the five furnishing functions, the archetypal materials or imagery which give form, and the atmospheric descriptors which afford a sense of the presence of mystery within the present sense of proper liturgical space. Applying that checklist, we find that the altar, according to Jungmann, is present only if it is brought in and placed before the stone seat for the presider. The throne for the book (lectern, ambo, pulpit) would have to be brought in also, unless there was no reading in these earliest liturgies. Baier suggests there must have been reading at the earliest liturgies, even at these memorials among the dead (David Baier, OFM, STD. Catholic Liturgies, trans. Richard Stapper, STD, St. Anthony Guild Press 1935, pg. 30) There is space as nave for the standing faithful. The walls make a round womb of the earth/tomb enclosure for the whole experience of the prayer.

There is profound silence, emptiness, darkness. Monumentality, afforded a dramatic reality in the depth below the surface within the very flesh of earth, almost consumes the pilgrim. Profusion, though not particularly evident in the "sanctuary" itself, is massed throughout the descent among the stacked resting places which line the walls of this descent of the living among the dead. That very descent evokes an inverted image of the mountain/city/temple, the progressive entry into the holy-of-holies, about which Eliade speaks so often and so eloquently.

The archetypes of stone and earth are in the very structure of the domus, although water and sky imagery are really quite distant. The wood of the tree would be evoked immediately when a table were taken in as altar and another as ambo.

So the cosmic center into which we have descended will also seem the cosmic pillar as soon as the species on the table would be consecrated. The body and blood of Christ is venerated and consumed within the midst of the Body of Christ. The "church militant" standing around the altar, within the bowels of mother earth, in the ritual presence of the "church triumphant," praying for the "church suffering" would undoubtedly fill the pilgrim with this sense of some holy ray going up and down from the center of the earth to the center of the universe.

Although we have very few opportunities to approach the eucharist in such a dramatic setting, it is not difficult to imagine it. There are places which capture a similar profound experience because of the dramatic setting chosen for building a church. Consider the Temppeliaukio Church in Helsinki. Built in 1961 by Timo and Tuomo Suomalainen (viewable in Edwin Heathcote and Iona Spens' Church Builders, Academy Editions, 1997, pp 98-101). This place built into the rock of a large town square, and entered through that rock, under a massive hovering dome, feels very much like the pilgrims are, somehow inside the earth while praying in the center of the city. There is another example in the hewn rock churches of Lalibela. Beta Ghiorghis (viewable in Judith Dupre. Churches. Harper

Collins, 2001, pp 40, 41) is entered by going down into the earth, into a hole dug around the exterior cruciform wall of the church. Very dark because of the small windows, this place is also an excellent example of Eliade's axis mundi, the cosmic pillar at the holy center. The earth itself feels like the flesh of the domus.

The Tomb of Gala Placidia

In Ravenna there is an ancient imperial tomb, built of brick in a patently evident cruciform elevation, like that at Beta Ghiorghis. The building dates back to an imperial presence before Justinian and Theodora whose palace here was to be the center in Italy for the Eastern emperors of the Roman Empire. The place was fabled, rich, and important when the imperial princess built this tomb for her family members. It is small for a church, has three sarcophagi in the arms of the cross-in-plan, leaving the western arm for entry and nave space. The altar would fit only in the center; the ambo would have to be brought in and there is so little space for the congregation that there seems no possibility of a throne for the presider.

However, this chapel is glorious in its decoration. In the Byzantine manner, there is nothing but alabaster backdrop where the living would congregate. The sarcophagi, too, are plain in color. The alabaster walls, flat and undisturbed on the inside actually have a paper-thin alabaster skin over the window apertures, so that there is this marvelously soft day light filtered into the chamber. The frame for all the living pilgrims, or the backdrop against which they would be seen is very plain while the barrel-vaulted ceiling, divided from the domed crossing by spandrels over the arches into the arms of the cross' ceiling, fairly glitters with polychrome mosaics. Images of the Good Shepherd, Saint Lawrence with his grill, doves and fountains are presided over by gold starred blue mosaic skies. The place is a little gem of Byzantine architecture and decoration.

How does it fare as a liturgical space? There is little room for altar, presider, pulpit, or even nave for a congregation. But for a very small worshiping community, this would be ideal. The archetypes are all present in the stone materials. The level plinth of the entire chapel, only a minimal surface depth higher than the earth of the garden outside the door, makes the earth quite evident. The fountains in the mosaic, the fire under Lawrence's grill, the starry vaults in the mosaics bring the water, fire, and sky right against the pilgrims face, as it were, as soon as the eyes can focus. The cosmic center is afforded by the crossing dome with its spiraling stars, giving a sense of center of the earth and pointer to the heavens right in the center of the building.

The atmospheric quality of silence is made serene by the thickness of the brick walls. Emptiness is made clear by the plane alabaster of the floor, wainscoting, and window glazing. Darkness prevails because there is only natural light filtered through a veil of alabaster slices adding to candle light. Profusion is afforded by repetitive images, stars, deer, fountains, doves, and the hundreds of thousands of mosaic tesserae which fills the higher walls and ceiling. Monumentality comes from the solid feel of the brick cruciform elevation. It has a weighty presence of those Ethiopian churches carved from the living rock.

The center of the universe seems a little distant because this place is so small. The entrance is directly from the outside, Eliade's profane space, to the inside, sacred space, without much transition, so the progressive entry and the mountain-city-temple archetype seem disemboweled. So the sense that the place is holy is very evident in some archetypes and atmospheric pointers but the furnishings and the space seem inadequate for a eucharistic liturgy of any size.

Although the tomb most probably was used for eucharistic liturgy. It is obviously not its main function. The glory of the decoration and the profound archetypal presences depicted do make of this building a significantly holy space. Its influence will be felt in many churches down the centuries.

The Basilica of Sant' Apollinare in Classe

The period after the "arrival" of Christianity into the imperial mindset is replete with new images of inculturation. Robes and gestures became part of the prerogative of the leaders of the political society at the discretion of the imperial court. (Baier, pg. 31, Jungmann, The Mass, pp. 62,63) Long after the impact of royal approval and noble patronage had become institutionalized the effects were still alive and thriving, if not healthy. Franco Zefferelli's Pope Innocent III, in the voice and visage of Sir Alec Guinness, could say to St. Francis of Assisi, "We are encrusted with power and jewels," with supreme bathos for the twentieth-century audience of

Brother Sun, Sister Moon. Comparatively Francis and his motley crew were free to do God's will. The pope blessed that freedom while he returned, trance-like to his throne, his triple tiara upheld by cardinal deacons, his copious cope straightened and supported by other acolytes. Up the mosaic steps he went, imperial, godly, inhabiting another world. We feel sorry for him.

Much of the "burden" was taken on in the fourth century when the empire saw political sagacity in granting the accoutrements of curial prestige to the bishops. Rings, shoes, colors, hats, cloaks, palium all came from imperial donation. They show up in the mosaics of Ravenna making the Christ not just a good shepherd but an imperial deity, worshipped by emperors and empresses (Justinian and Theodora at both San Vitale and Sant' Apollinare Nuovo) and sitting on imperial throne with imperial pillow and imperial robes and, ——and his mother does likewise. The ecumenical councils which established the canonical credal formulae were just about finished when this period began. Jesus, God and Man is eternal, His authority proceeding from the Father. There never was a time when He was not. All of creation was created in and for Him. His mother is mother of both the human and the divine; she is the theotokos, the Mother-of-God. Those who disagreed with decreed matters of faith and brought disruption to the empire were subject to imperial discipline.

Jungmann says that the imperial accoutrements come to the Church as a

> ...reverberation of the Christological disturbances which the Greek Orient suffered. In this we must see the chief factor which explains the difference between the Byzantine world and the Greek world of primitive Christianity...other factors—national characteristics, political absolutism and above all caesaropapism..." (Pastoral Liturgy, pg. 10)

This is also the time when Liturgy begins to be a large public ritual for which emperors and governors build great halls. Those large gathering places in the Roman world had been the basilicas, the halls where the representatives of the ruler, the basileus (in court Greek), sat in judgment of legal cases, or where imperial decrees were presented to the people. These buildings are large enough to accommodate the now large crowds who comprise the assembly, the ecclesia. They are soon adapted and basilicas for use of the Church are built. St. Peter's old Basilica was built by imperial funds leveling the Vatican Hill, filling in the Circus Maximus, burying the cemeteries, to the specifications of an imperial decree. St. Paul's-outside-the-walls, St. John Lateran, St. Mary Major soon followed, immense structures with images of imperial Godhead and imperial heavenly court in mosaic at the eastern apses.

Sant' Apollinare in Classe is a good basilica for us to look at because it is early and well preserved. It gives us an insight into the beginnings of large ritual spaces for the post Hebraic era in the western Church.

The eastern emperor, Justinian, intended to move to the great growing metropolis of Ravenna. The city, soon after the time of Justinian and Theodora, had become a city of former glory leaving almost intact the treasures of its two baptisteries, two important tomb chapels, imperial chapel, and three basilicas. Peter Hammond says that the basilica, a Roman imperial building, was originally chosen because of its convenient suitability not because of its beauty. (Peter Hammond, Liturgy and Architecture, Columbia University Press. 1961, pg. 8)

The basilica of Sant' Apollinare in Classe is found almost free of context because the canal city which surrounded it silted up and became earthbound centuries ago. It is, therefore, without major additions or subtractions since the time of its construction.

Entering through a rather plain but generous courtyard, one would originally have encountered a font or well which Jungmann claims would normally stand in the atrium of a Christian basilica (Missarum Solemnia Vol II. Pg.77). This basilica has two side aisles created by single rows of marble monoliths. The terra cotta colored brick walls are softly pink but barely penetrated by alabaster covered windows; this light is very soft! The nave is taller than the two side aisles, or ambulatories, which are lighted by similar alabastered lights and roofed with a peaked, wooden, lean-to roof. The east end of the great hall is cupped by a semi-domed apse covered with mosaic images, mostly a very rich, soft chromium-colored, green background with simple representations of apostles and bishops at the lower level between the five large divided lights (alabastered openings with a wood or iron grid of internal support. Above this is a symbolic representation of the saint, Apollinarus, as a shepherd with a flock of sheep. Above this is a more symbolic representation of the Transfiguration, two Old Testament figures floating in clouds on either side of the

Transfigured, symbolically represented in a lapis-colored cross (without a corpus), before the gaze of three sheep (the apostles, Peter, James, and John). Outside the rounded arch of the apse, on the proscenium wall, are twelve sheep ascending a curve to the pinnacle of the peaked roof, where there is a Christ bust in benediction, a pantocrator, This title, meaning "maker of all," unites the Son with the Father, according to conciliar documents which make the three members of the Trinity co-eval in there eternal existence, never beginning and never ending. To his side are the four symbols of the evangelists. Other than this rich, east wall decoration, the basilica has only rondels of the bishops of Rome in a frieze on the architrave over the spandrels of the arcade.

At the base of the apsidal wall of the exedra, the raised eastern platform, is a banc of seats running the course of the curve. The seat seems to be for a whole presbyteral group. In front of this banc is a stone altar. The seats and the altar are on the raised plinth of the exedra; before them on the floor of the nave sits a stone bema, within which is an important relic. It would serve very well as the throne for the book but the reading should take place in the middle of the apse so that the sound box shape might send the voice over the heads of the congregation and down to even those at the back of the crowd, So, this bema is probably not the place for the book. It cannot be an altar, according to Jungmann who asserts that there was never a second altar in a church for the first five hundred years. (Public Worship, pg. 61)

So, there is no ambo, though the fourth century sacramentaries indicate that there were lectionaries for the reading of the different texts of the Sacred Scriptures, epistola and evangelium, to be read during the Sunday liturgies by different ministers. One can imagine the reading from the steps of the sanctuary but there is no permanent place for this; perhaps again portable lecterns were in vogue. Perhaps, on the other hand indeed, the lower stand is an example of the bema from the synagogue. It was a raised reading altar for the East Syrian Liturgy.

The nave is vast and open, for the people. This is how the people would have gathered in an imperial basilica. The term "basilica" comes from basileus, court Greek for the emperor, and oikos, court Greek for house. The basilica in the administrative scheme of the emperor was his house among the provinces or among the people. It was where the representative of the imperium, the power of the empire, stood over the people to render judgements or decree the will of the emperor. In the new dispensation the will of the heavenly Emperor is in the sacred scriptures. So these basilican churches were the house of the God of the Good News of revelation where the eucharist took place. The nave is enclosed by a profusion of columns, windows, papal images, beams of the peaked roof. The apsidal hemidome seems to bay out from the people's place, so that all are enclosed within a single domus. The unity of the place is profoundly noticeable to even the casual visitor. It seems appropriate for today's liturgy.

The archetype of stone is evident in the walls, altar, bema, seat, and columns. The floor seems contiguous with the earth, so the archetype of being planted on the earth seems apparent; it is reinforced by the green mosaic ground throughout the eastern wall. The archetype of water is found in the forecourt fountain but it would be profoundly reinforced by the waterways that originally flowed in canals throughout this seaside port. The sky is evident in the mosaics, again, but the alabaster divided light windows are much larger and admit much more sky into the vast chamber than the windows of the other basilicas in town, Sant' Apollinare Nuovo and San Francesco, or the tomb, the imperial chapel, or the baptisteries. The monumentality is tangible in the vastness of the space and the height and weight of the roof. The mountain-city-temple of progressive entry is engaged by the outer court and inner narthex, but the raised eastern exedra fairly sings that this is the holy place within this church.

Silence and emptiness are mitigated hardly at all by the visual delights in the mosaics. The quiet city is hardly a threat to either. The windows admit a lot of filtered light. The dark ceiling and the recesses of the aisle roof, however, define a mysterious place for saints and angels to cavort with the spirits of the congregants.

So this place seems quite appropriate for large eucharistic liturgical rituals even today but the focus implied in the plan of the space is reinforced by the visual aids of the mosaics. The place is inviting to anyone who would meditate here alone, even though it is so vast. I think it is the focus afforded by the face of Christ, a kind of pantocrator at the apex of the proscenium arch wall, reinforced by the powerful image of the cross on an azure/turquoise field, a profoundly non-threatening presence, representing a godly Christ without fearsome features. The bishops and sheep/apostles also make for a comfortable welcome on the wall which virtually embraces every pilgrim.

Decoration in the Early Period

Both Jungmann and Lowrie assert that all the Christian art of the earliest centuries was about death and afterlife. Jungmann says it all had an "eschatological quality" (Pastoral Liturgy, pg. 4). Lowrie says "...the pictured decoration of the catacombs referred predominantly, if not exclusively, to the themes which were associated with death or rather with the Christian hope which illuminated it"(Monuments fo the Early Church, pg. 47). The images in Gala Placidia's tomb are more flamboyant than the simple murals of the catacombs. There is a courtly quality to the opulence and to the arrangements of fountains, pennants, stars, rondels, deer and doves, foliated framing, etc. The Good Shepherd is certainly about the presence of Christ to the living and not only as the judge of the dead. So in the few short centuries the imagery has changed from simple faith reminders about the divinity of Christ and the need for living right, to the humanity of Christ and the need for living well. The wealth and power of empire slip into the next phase of church architecture quite easily.

The decoration of the upper quadrant of the space, the ceiling environment, is totally different from the congregational backdrop. The almost blank alabaster screen against which all visitors would be viewed, renders the closest peers visually in balance with the heavenly glories which sit in their bejeweled flat world.

The decorated upper environs become a cliché of Byzantine architecture. It is copied in the basilicas of the early Roman Catholic culture. St. Paul's-outside-the-walls, St. John Lateran, Santa Maria Maggiore, San Clemente are more classically Roman examples of this Byzantine style which was epitomized in Ravenna's basilicas, Saint Apollinaris, Nuovo and in Classe, and the imperial chapel of San Vitale, plus the Orthodox and Arian baptisteries. The style shows in the Baptistery of Florence, the doge's palace chapel in Venice, San Marco and, later at Cefalu and Monreale in Sicily, later still, in the new cathedral of St. Louis in Missouri, and even in the Cathedral Basilica of the Immaculate Conception. So the designs of Gala Placidia, initiated in Roman Constantinople, but spread to the west through Ravenna, become an international benchmark of riches spent on the house of God. Sometimes the decoration takes over, sometimes it is in its rightful place. The Church of St. Robert Bellarmine in modern Rome, a domed dark modern church has a dark green-blue mosaic sky as its ceiling. It cannot compare with the yellow greens of Ravenna or the golds of Venice or Constantinople. But the point is that a decorating principle which was born in an imperial culture became a norm, a preference, a way of stating the "arrival" of the Catholics into the "pagan" world which we inhabit. The motif develops into a style and can transmogrify into a stagnant cliché. The preference becomes, in other words, sometimes more a statement about how important the congregants are than how glorious is their God. We will consider this polarity more when we discuss Bernard and Suger in the Medieval church.

Actually the images of God, Jesus, and the heavenly court had begun to resemble the courtly images of the Byzantine imperial court soon after the Edict of Milan which allowed in 313 CE the practice of the Faith throughout the imperial realms. Malraux says, however, "What was meant by 'beauty' in fifth century art had nothing in common with what it meant in later periods. It revealed man's awareness of the essentially divine nature of the gods and its basic difference from the human." (Andre Malraux., The Metamorphosis of the Gods, trans. Gilbert Stuart, Doubleday. 1960, pg. 64) Gerardus van der Leeuw speaks of the "...the awe-inspiring divine orge, that about the holy which excites fear," and "a nuance of the awe-inspiring...the ghostly, the ghastly." He says that "We come still closer to the holy through the influence of darkness and semi-darkness...through the impenetrable darkness is indicated the fact that the deity 'dwells in unapproachable light.'" (Sacred and Profane Beauty, pp. 190-192).

So these images of the heavenly are big headed, strange colored, hieratically stiff. And yet, they command a profound engagement, one which has moved into fresco as in the early Romanesque painting at Léon in Spain or Russian Late Medieval masterpieces at the czars' cathedrals within the Kremlin. This "divine orge" has a long and prestigious history both in the west and in the east.

The use of mosaic became an awe-inspiring indicator of the wealth and power of those who employ it. In Saint Peter's Basilica and Saint Isaac's in Saint Petersburg, the mosaic tesserae are so miniscule as to deceive the viewer at first into thinking the artwork is a masterpiece of Renaissance exuberance in oils. The shock of realization evokes an appreciation of the scientific and technical ability to transform a fully-realized, fluid work of art into a cartoon for the (exorbitantly expensive) finished product.

Prelude to the Next Period

There are many different texts of liturgical rubrics which could apply in these Ravennese churches but differences in prayer texts reflect different theological prerogatives established in credal formulae and conciliar agreements at Nicaea (325), Constantinople (381), Ephesus (431), and Chalcedon (451). The variations are in consequence of particular emphases intended with regard to the divinity of Christ, the separation of the persons of the Trinity, or the relationship of the Virgin- Mother to the God-Man. The thread of humility, before the divinity, however, begins to be notieceable in the fabric of the medieval theological tapestry. The Basilian Liturgy, attributed to Basil the Great (d. 379) has the priest referring to the people as "lowly and sinful and unworthy slaves." (Jungmann, Missarum Solemnia Vol I, pg.38) The growth of this sense of unworthiness is closely related to what Jungmann sees as a change in the very concept of the Eucharist:

> In the earlier periods of liturgical life we saw the emphasis placed on the Mass as a eucharistia, a prayer of thanks from the congregation who were invited to participate by a Gratias agamus, and whose gifts, in the course of the Mass, were elevated by the word of the priest into a heavenly sacrificial offering. But now an opposite view was taking precedence in men's minds, swayed as they were especially by the teaching of Isidore of Seville. The Eucharist is the bona gratia, which God grants to us, and which at the climactic moment of the Mass, the consecration, descends to us. Soon scholars were earnestly at work trying to discover when, precisely in the Mass-Liturgy this descent took place. (Missarum Solemnia Vol I, pg.38)

This place is, therefore, the scene of protestations of humility in the presence of great and dignified exhibitions of wealth and power. There are great processionsand high seats for the hierarchy which stressed, for this communal commemoration of the Banquet of the Lord, in the trappings of imperial authority, the difference between us and them. On the one hand, humans have levels of nobility. On the other, the dignity of the heavenly court is of a wholly other magnitude. Perhaps, this schizophrenia about class worth is inappropriate in the Church but this place is certainly appropriate for the "public work" of this newly-arrived people: appropriate both as the expression of a people's aspirations and of its relationship to the Christ of the mysterium.

Chapter Three: The Medieval Church

Fall and Rise

The development of the Roman Church after the first centuries was greatly dependent on its status within the Roman Empire. The stability of all of Europe was dependent on the condition of the Empire as well. So the churches which developed within the "Middle Ages" were expressions of what was going on within the Empire and indicators of the aspirations of the Christian peoples of the Empire to take their places within a community of peoples. The Fall of Rome, of course, changes everything.

The fact that Rome has a number of ways of falling (and different places and times for its many "falls") has substantial impact on how the people get up and get up again, and again, and again. The role of bishop being transformed into a leadership role in "Christendom" is countered by the growth of monasticism and its consequent political realities. The bishops come into conflict with the temporal leaders of the various peoples who rise from the ashes of one or another conflagration. The loss of imperial status for a city and the rising hegemony of new nobles, from both old imperial families and from new tribal chieftans and their successors, is a fluid political base for the rising edifice we call the Middle Ages. The churches of the Middle Ages are built, at first, of "spare parts" after the ruin of the old culture, combined with new inventions of the differing ascendancies within new political realities.

William Lethaby, in <u>Architecture, Mysticism and Myth</u> (Braziller, 1979, pg. 42) tells us there are only two kinds of plan for church buildings. Throughout history the circle and the rectangle, the round and the long plan dominate. There have been, of course, crosses, spheres and cubes, and even fish and ship shapes to plans and elevations. But Lethaby's conclusion is inarguably reasonable.

In the earliest years of Christendom there were round spaces which were, often enough modeled after the imperial round temple for a multitude of gods. The Pantheon was designed so that none of the gods would be jealous of the preeminence given to the one whose altar seemed to be at the long end of the sanctuary. During the Greek and Roman periods, the temples were typically long chambers behind a columned portico, with the naos, the sacred interior, focused on the statue of the god for whom the temple was built. The Parthenon, with Phidias' chryselephantine Athena Parthenos, holding within its tons of gold and ivory, the very treasury of the city, is the prime analogate for all those temples built in classical Greece and Rome. The Solomonic Temple of Jerusalem was similarly oriented, with forecourts, pillared entrance, and a central cella where the holy-of-holies was the repository of the Ark of the Covenant.

The round plan of the Roman Pantheon of the Flavian imperial family was an ingenious innovation. It did, however, profoundly affect temple architecture in the west thereafter, because it was so grand and so beautiful with its great height, its magnificent coffered dome with its oculus open to the sky, and its mysterious centering effect which affects all its visitors, even today.

Among those round spaces were a couple of chapels built with imperial funds, motivated by imperial aspirations. The Hagia Sophia and Hagia Irene of Constantine (and their later replacements built under Justinian's rule) are immense and beautiful, even in the ruined state in which we find them today, after centuries outside the care of the Christian Church. The Palace Chapel of San Vitale, octogonal in its elevation is really a rounded space inside. The octogan of Charlemagne's chapel at Aachen quite pointedly looks to those Constantinopolitan predecessors for inspiration.

All of those places mentioned above, however, have not a central plan when considering the liturgical focus. Today each of those round places has an altar at the eastern end, with the sanctuary at one end of the circular space. Baptisteries, like the ones in Ravenna, both the Arian and Orthodox, the ones in Pisa and Florence, or the one at St. John Lateran, have a central liturgical flow plan. These, however, were all built to celebrate the initiatory rites of the Sacrament of Baptism. For the eucharistic liturgy they each have, today, an altar facing the eastern wall and a baptismal pool in the center—good really, for one focal ritual of passage with a kind of eucharistic accompaniment, as a side-show of sorts.

So, we have this prinicpal about the design of churches, namely, that there are only round or long churches. But we have a contradictory history. This contradiction is carried into the modern era with the eastern apsidal sanctuaries of the great domes of the modern era: St Mary of the Flowers in Florence, St. Peter's Basilica in Rome, St. Paul's in London, and St. Isaac's in St. Petersburg. Even Latrobe's St. Mary's Cathedral in Baltimore has this conflict in plan and elevation.

A Question

So , the idea that there could be a round plan. What is it? What does it imply that would make it architecturally so compelling? Why is it liturgically so reviled? In fact, the Second Vatican Council claims the centrality of the eucharist and proposes the actual physical centering of the sacramental presence between the priest and the people, going so far as to imply, for many Catholic leaders, that a human backdrop to the eucharist is preferable to an artistic one.

In the Middle Ages, the Church became one of the central arms of power in the world. The priesthood of the patriarchs evolved into the hegemony of the hierarchs. The central seats of liturgy became centers of culture and power, commerce and education during the last days of the Empire. Then they became prizes for those who would aspire to power rivaling the emperors. There were political roles for the leaders of the many different factions of power. Counts, dukes, marechals, and kings came from tribal groups and old imperial centers alike. The new nobility fought its way to the top of the heap and worked hard at maintaining position, power, and wealth enough to establish bases of power which would be passed to future generations.

In the growth of the Church as the spiritual center of Christendom, a new class was established by the development of monasticism. Benedict and his sister, Scholastica, in the seventh century codified a movement which resulted in great religious houses all across the face of Christendom, religious houses where peace reigns by rule, libraries thrive through study, and population centers arise through stability. Duchesses soon vie with abbesses for power in the world. The great religious houses find a way to consolidate power in the tenth century through the Cluniac reforms and the subsequent organization of systems of monastic rule. Augustinian, Cistercian, Franciscan, Dominican, and Carmelite rules arise as the most profoundly influential and long lasting monastic systems, not added to until the Renaissance foundations of Jesuits, Theatines, Oratorians. They bring about another way for the organization of the economic, political, and ethical reality which was becoming modern Europe.

The cathedral was the image of the authority of the bishops. The abbey church that for the monastic liege lords (and ladies). Both arms of the Church, the abbey and the cathedral, had temporal power to rival that of the castle, manor, and palace of the nobles and royals. Everybody was Christian in this Europe, unless they were infidels, pagans, or Jews. The building of churches was quite different from the forms just after the legitimacy began, under the old imperial aegis. The need to protect the citizens against the military might of rival factions made the churches into fortresses, both virtual and actual, so that one lord's armed ambition could be fended off by another's fortifications!

Chapter Four:
Romanesque to Gothic

The Romanesque Church

A number of things show up in churches during the Middle Ages that have no real meaning in theology or spirituality. The altar rail, the monstrance, even the unleavened disc of bread, choir stalls with their misericordes, cancellerias for singing of the Gregorian Chant, rood screens, iconostases for the Eastern Rite churches, all of these developments have reasons for coming into common usage. They are culturally established but peripheral to the central mystery of the Church.

There are some political realities which arise from the circumstances of life in post imperial Europe. Fiefs and vassalage attend feudal success. This means that a successful count or prior comes to control more land as his territorial responsibilities grow with the inheritance of dowry rights or the re-assignment of fiefdoms after battles won and lost. The whole baffling system of accountabilities grows more and more "byzantine" as alliances are made and rules are laid down to preserve the peace ——or the pieces of property.

The churches, at the outset of what we have come to call the Romanesque Era in architecture, are what is built of bits and pieces of architecture left after the disappearance of the prosperity and protection which prevailed under the praetorian system. The churches are built as fortresses in many instances to protect against plague, pillage, and plunder.

The building techniques of the Romans, as well as their ruins are employed. So there are brick and concrete, the arches, small windows, and barrel vaulting. The development of the rood and altar rail apparently had something to do with the separation of the feudal liege lord's authority from that of the clergy in conjunction with the bishop and the Roman papacy. The part of the feudal chapel outside the rail was under the jurisdiction of the lord of the manor and that inside belonged to that of the Church, which came to mean the central authority. There were choirs for the communal gathering of the resident subset of authoritative church persons; canons, monks, nuns, all would sing and pray from their special chambers, filled later with misericordes , elaborate choir stalls with carved backs and folding alternatives to sitting or standing, almost thrones in some places.

Torcello

From the seventh to the eleventh century the cathedral of Torcello was built on an island which was the original seat of the Venetian Republic. Like Sant' Apollinare in Classe, this building's past is truncated by the vicissitudes of the sea, the silt, and the political reality which needed to protect a city center from invasion. So Venice moved to Rialto, the hard bank, of a river near where Piazza San Marco was soon born. The older city center was abandoned, to survive for us, rather pristine in its eleventh century Romanesque stasis.

The basilica is today entered through a side portico but in its heyday the main portal was through a forecourt which had a baptistery, now a ruin with a classical capital hollowed as a well. The pilgrim entering the original main portal comes through a porch and, on entry, has behind him or her, a large mosaic depicting the Last Judgement. It covers the whole wall but is an object of attention only when the visitor is leaving. The two aisles have tomb monuments in their shadowed recesses but they date from a much later period than the original structure. The floor, now a mosaic of large pieces of marble, had been a foot lower and made of black and white mosaic in the classical Roman style. There is a large climb-in pulpit to the left of a choir space which is fenced in by a marble wall. Both the pulpit and wall are covered in ill-fitted marble slabs, obviously taken from some other place for which they were cut. Over the entrance to the choir is a wooden rood screen with a very large three-figured crucifixion, dark with age. This ominously fills the space above; it is set against a background of a peaked, wooden roof similar to the ones at Sant' Apollinare in Classe, Sant' Apollinare Nuovo, and San Francesco in Ravenna. The apse behind the choir is filled with stepped marble benches; in the center of these rows of seats, at the very center of the apse is a throne, The open half-dome of the apse is similar in structure to the one at the Ravenna basilicas but it is repeated to the left and the right by the apsidal ends of the side aisles (similar to only Sant' Apollinare in Classe). The one at the right has a mosaic of the Christ in Benediction, on a gold background. This is the oldest mosaic in the place and is probably similar to the one which must have preceded the one now in the central apsidal hemidome.That one is now a black-robed standing madonna reflecting a later Middle Ages development.

The Virgin Assumed (even on earth)

There is during the Middle Ages an iconographic shift from the Last Judgment to the Crucifixion and from the conquering archangel Michael to the gentle Virgin and Queen. It is interesting that in the cathedral of Torcello there is a powerful Last Judgment on the west wall of the interior and a peaceful Virgin Orans in the apsidal hemidome. Henry Adams explains:

> Men were, after all, not wholly inconsequent; their attachment to Mary rested on an instinct of self-preservation. They knew their own peril. If there was to be a future life, Mary was their only hope. She alone represented Love, The Trinity were, or was, One, and could, by the nature of its essence, administer justice alone. Only childlike illusion could expect a personal favor from Christ. Turn the dogma as one would, to this it must logically come. Call the three Godheads by what names one liked, still they must remain One; must administer one justice; must admit only one law. In that law, no human weakness or error could exist; by its essence it was infinite, eternal, immutable. There was no crack and no cranny in the system, through which human frailty could hope for escape. One was forced from corner to corner by a remorseless logic until one fell helpless at Mary's feet. (Henry Adams. Mont-Saint-Michel and Chartres, New American Library; A Mentor Book, 1961, pg. 246)

Adams says that this happened at the same time as when the Christians of Europe preferred to seek the aid of the maternal against the evils of the period, what Barbara Tuchman calls the three-fold evils of "plague, pillage, and taxes." (A Distant Mirror, Ballantine Books, 1978, pg. 580) Adams says that St. Michael, the archangel of war had been replaced between the building of Mont-Saint-Michel and Notre Dame de Chartres. Sir Kenneth Clark states with his characteristic certitude that::

> The earliest cult figure of the Virgin and Child of any size is a painted wooden statue in St. Denis which must date from about 1130. The great Romanesque churches were dedicated to the saints

> whose relics they contained—St. Sernin, St. Etienne, St. Lazarus, St. Denis, St. Mary Magdalene—none of them to the Virgin. Then after Chartres the greatest churches in France were dedicated to her—Paris, Amiens, Laon, Rouen, Rheims. (Civilization: A Personal View, Harper and Row, 1969, pg. 58)

At any rate, this late Virgin of Torcello is similar in design and execution to the madonnas of San Marco, the center of the Republic, built and decorated during the six centuries following the exodus from Torcello.

This place is much darker than any of the baslicas of Ravenna. The windows are small and very high. The theme of unworthiness seems to have taken firm root in the consciousness of this people. The fenced-off place of the altar and the constant reminder of the cross before the image of the hovering mother set the tone for the congregation but the liturgy is still a dialogue between the clerical class seated behind the sanctuary, the people in the choir, and the people in the nave proper

Are there appropriate furnishings in this place? There is a pulpit. It is not from the original foundation of the church, but probably was built after the outbreak of preaching which began to flourish after the thirteenth-century monastic foundations based their mission in preaching. Especially is this true of the mendicant orders following the Rules of St. Francis of Assisi and St. Dominic. The altar is also a later addition. It is of stone and placed at the front of the fenced-in sanctuary for mass facing the people. Jungmann says that the fencing of the altar has to do with its becoming more and more aloof, an architectonic expression of an intellectual development (Missarum Solemnia Vol I, pg. 256) He also says that after the twelfth century it became necessary that the altar be of stone and immovable (Public Worship, pg.61); it remained so until after the post-conciliar developments after Vatican II. The throne is set in the center of the presbyteral banc lining the rear wall of the apse.

The clerical area and the choir are separated from the space of the laity by the strong visual block of the rood screen. So the domus is divided. The rood, in fact, is massive and so high that the congregation must bend the head back to see it, thus it does not point to the eucharist, does not focus, but distracts. This arrangement is most inappropriate even on viewing the space without a liturgy.

This basilica is a good example of early Romanesque buildings because it is a hodge-podge of temporal and practical revisions, but done in a manner that indicates a community on the edge, things are done with slip-shod transitions, sometimes with finesse. San Clemente, Santa Sabina, Santa Maria in Cosmedin, all still have this sense of many parts organized into a not-so-coherent whole.

The atmospheric influences are these. Silence is maintained in a way similar to the previously mentioned basilicas; the variety of surfaces, the number of muffling surfaces, including the wooden roof and the various sound-catching corners under the eaves of the side aisles. Dark, with few and small windows way up in the clerestory, the small space seems quite cluttered.

Stone is in the altar, the floor, the sanctuary rails, the clerical bench and the throne, the pillars. The tree at the center of the earth, the axis mundi, is certainly revered in the immense rood. The destroyed baptistery in the forecourt, still represents water's life-giving presence. Here, too, the ever present lagoon is almost a personal presence itself. The gold of the mosaics symbolizes the ethereal sky. The earth seems to be right below the floor. The mountain-city-temple is experienced by the progressive entry and the raised eastern apse.

There is little sense of profusion. The monumentality is lent by a sense of immanent doom rather than massive structures held in spiritual tension. But the absence of a living community is not only symbolized in the grotesque full-body relics on the right wall of the nave; the whole place seems dessicated. More a museum than a church, it feels dead.

There is a confusion in the place. Partly ruin, partly restoration, partly repository of wondrous remains from different periods in the life of this particular island place, it is better appreciated as a museum.

Santa Fosca

Right next door to the old cathedral is the charming little church of Santa Fosca. Built in the eleventh century, it seems a perfect example of the round church that Lethaby speaks of. However, it, too, like San Vitale and the Carolingian chapel at Aachen has a cruciform (long) plan and an octogonal (round) elevation. The porch entry is inviting, the brick walls are simple, the terrazzo floor very warm. The table altar in marble, the small wooden pulpit, the spare wooden benches, all within the Greek cross plan with each arm barrel-vaulted and plastered. The round central dome is wood, the monolithic columns are soft white marble. The rood beam at the entrance to the little apse is low enough so that the cross seems to occupy a rightful place within the sanctuary. It focuses the congregation without competing with the priest. Everything seems to be taken care of with loving hands. The reality of something alive in this place makes a completely different impression from the dried out atmosphere of the cathedral next door.

This little gem has all the elements necessary for an appropriate liturgical space. The main characteristic of care for the place has a profound effect. The place is sacred to someone and so s/he takes care of it. The uncared for museum next door is not without its charms but this sense of careful "attention to detail" (John Dewey's phrase from Art as Experience (Minton Balch, 1934) by which he denotes the artist, is clearly appealing in the smaller chapel.

Santo Stefano Rotondo

Santo Stefano Rotondo is an anomaly in that it was actually built in the round, with the sanctuary in the center. Today, with its medieval decoration gone and its central sanctuary outlined by innumerable monolithic marble columns in a double colonnade, this church is a formidable "white box." There is a central altar table of marble and a short wall around the sanctuary hiding what might be a place for a presidential seat and a portable pulpit. The place is spare and without any images but it is absolutely focused. The only trouble seems to be that there is nothing to rest the eyes on, no place to look except at the altar and the priest who is praying for me. The problem here is a problem with many renovations after the Second Vatican Council. In concentrating on the priesthood of the people, rather than simply on the priesthood of the ordained, and, in the same mode concentrating on the integrity of the eucharist present among the praying people-of-God, the designers have had no truck with the imagination of the individual human being who might belong to the congregation. There is consideration only for a profoundly disengaged meditative correspondent who would concentrate on the simplest of mysteries and on the interpersonal dialogue with the priest and the other members of the congregation. The pillars are lovely, the space is profoundly holy, but there is no food for any part of the person except the linear intellect and the most austere of aesthetic sensibilities. This is, perhaps, the primordial white box, this Santo Stefano Rotondo.

Liturgies

There were very many different liturgical formulas-at-large during the time when the Romanesque developed. Jungmann lists the East Syrian Liturgy which developed, at first, from Palestinian Aramaic (in the Nestorian and Chaldean community). He describes the Latin mass as having two types at first: the Roman-African and the Gallic, the latter eventually developing into the Gallican, Celtic, Mozarabic ("old Spanish"), and Ambrosian (Milanese). He lists, too, the fourth-century Clementine Liturgy (established and enlarged by St. John Chrysostom) from the eighth book of the Apostolic Constitutions (<u>Missarum Solemnia Vol I</u>, pg 35 ff); the Basilian Liturgy of Basil the Great (d 379) (ibid, pg. 38); the Mystagogic Catechesis of Cyril of Jerusalem (d 386), describing the West-Syrian Liturgy incorporating the anaphora of St. James (centered first in Antioch and later in Jerusalem) (ibid, pg. 41 ff); the Greek "Liturgy of St. Mark" (established at Alexandria), the Euchologian of Serapion; and the Byzantine Liturgy of St. John Chrysostom, the fourth century Antiochene Mass (ibid, pg 41 ff) and the eleventh century Romano-Frankish liturgy in the Mainz Pontifical spread through the travels of Otto the Great (ibid. pg. 95)..

All of the liturgies mentioned have their own flavor but the eastern ones tended to have a more mysterious attitude toward the "confection of the sacrament," an attitude which is evidenced today in the iconostasis of the Eastern Churches, first reported in 563 CE. (Baier, pg. 200)

Basilica San Marco

This palace chapel of sorts, belonging to the state ceremonial and court building of the Republic of Venice, was a chapel for the Doge. Its liturgical practices were probably more eastern than western for most of its millennium of existence.

> The building of St. Mark's is linked with a legend, according to which the evangelist St. Mark was shipwrecked on the Adriatic at a place corresponding to present-day Venice. As he came to land an angel appeared to him and told him that his body would one day be interred on that spot. The Venetians took this prediction to heart and in 828 they brought St. Mark's body from Alexandria and began building a church which was to bear his name. (Munemoto Yanagi, Eiichi Takahashi, Shigebumi Tsuji, and Yasushi Nagatsuka, trans. Nicholas Fry, Byzantium, Chartwell Books, 1978, pg.124)

This church, the repository of the pride of the Serene Republic and of the aspirations of the doges, is, in the story above, a benchmark for myth-making and for excuse-fabrication. The myth is that St. Mark was foretold of this reliquary sanctuary long before it was chosen by the victimized citizens of the former Roman colonial city as a place of refuge from invading hoards of Ostrogoths, Vandals, Huns, and the like. This becomes the reason for stealing the body and building an honorable place for pilgrimage.

After all, the Middle Ages are also marked by this growing sense that there is power in the other world where God, the Blessed Mother, and saints reside. Remember Eliade's kratophany? Power expressing itself demands our respect. The power can save us victims of plague or pillage. The cathedrals and monasteries become places where all the nobles can bank spiritual treasure. They can also bank economic futures on the next couple of centuries of monument making and the hordes of paying pilgrims who will pray where Mary's girdle resides (Chartres), or the Magdalen's hair (Vezeley), or the Crown of Thorns (the Sainte Chapelle),. The bodies of the patriarchs also have stellar properties for healing and other miracles. Peter is in Rome at the basilica built by Constantine to house his relics, Paul is supposedly also in his own basilica, James is in Sant' Iago de Compostella near the Portuguese border in Spain, Denis is at Monmartre, Augustine is at Canterbury.

The Disneyland of today was the pilgrimage church and town of that great dark age. The difference may, of course, be that the Mouse cannot ask God for miracles, cannot intercede for the living at the throne of the Eternal. Be that as it may, the saint prayed to at a pilgrimage site might just hear the prayers, even though the mythological presence might be fabricated. And so, San Marco becomes a great treasury of the valuable spoils of Venetian mercantile prowess and naval might.

Appropriateness of San Marco as a domed church

From the gracious, and often crowded and bustling, Piazza San Marco the pilgrim enters the five-portaled Westfront under glowing mosaics of the mythological translation of the body of the apostle to this reliquary. Except for the northernmost and oldest portal tympanum, done in the hieratic Byzantine style, these tympana are motion-filled Baroque pictures. Under the unfurled robes caught in a constant flurry by the mosaic artists, the pilgrim passes into a more and more hieratic and mysterious, dark world. Jeannette Mirsky, describing the domes of another great church of the Byzantine world, Hagia Sophia in Istanbul, says that Procopius "spoke of 'its golden dome, which seems to rest not on solid masonry but is as if suspended from heaven to cover the space.'" (<u>Houses of God</u>, Viking Press 1965, pg. 217) Malraux, describing the same Hagia Sophia declares, "The Byzantines visualized a divine space permeating earthbound space as the light of a taper permeates the darkness. The divine space was vaguely associated with the universe, since the East imagined the firmament as an enormous cupola." (Malraux, pg. 136) The vaults of the narthex of St. Mark's are covered with a pandemonium of religious and heavenly events, some in the domed vaults, arranged in the mandala form common to the Byzantine style. These are older and less mannerist than their counterparts on the west front.In <u>Buddhism: The Illustrated Guide</u> (Kevin Trainor, Ed. Oxford, 2001, pp. 88, 89), Michael Willis describes the Buddhist penchant for mandalas. It seems that the circular motif is a centering device used as prayer and meditation, making sand paintings, or three dimensional sculptures, even temple sized domes within square frames and with tower. He mentions specifically "the magnificent ninth century structure at Borobudur in Java." He describes something that has visual representation in Navaho painting and Mayan temple structures.

Yanagi et al. in <u>Byzantium</u> claim a constant in the dome with the four smaller domes as an eastern motif showing itself in Russia in the cubic elevation with five domes, as in the Kremilin cathedrals. Dupre (<u>Churches</u>, pg. 67) cites the traditional stave church blended with Byzantine influences as an adaptation with higher and higher pinnacled domes, like what St. Basil's in Red Square finally becomes in its most recent renovations. Actually called the Cathedral of the Intercession of the Mother of God, this church originally built for Ivan the Terrible, claims in brick and mortar the relationship that his grandfather, Ivan III, had secured through marriage to the Paleologue princess Sophia. The "right" to call Moscow the "Third Rome," after Constantinople, seemed logical. The interesting relationship of domed edifices to imperial dreams finds fitting proclamation in Alexander the First's Cathedral of St. Isaac in St. Petersburg or Napoleon's being buried in Louis XIV's magnificent domed Church of Saint Louis des Invalides at the soldiers' hospital.

This San Marco also has a three-dimensional mandala dome with four smaller domes. It also has dreams of grandeur but not of being the imperial city, since Venice is defiantly republican, remaining free and independent long enough to be the oldest republic in the memory of mankind. And yet the cathedral and the city are full of treasures which proclaim that Venetians thought themselves better than any imperial civilization that ever existed. With no forests and no quarries, la Serenissima is a more-than-substantial city built with booty and loot stolen from the biggest and richest and most powerful cities in Europe. The Serene Republic also outlasted all of them in independence and surpassed most in culture.

So, on into the cathedral of the patriarch of Venice, who is not and never was a patriarch in any ecclesiastical sense of the word. In fact the cathedral is only now the seat of a bishop. For most of its life it was the chapel of the Doge's Palace.

Up the steps into the nave, the pilgrim ascends into the upper and inner reaches of the sanctuary, always mindful of the domes and arches bathed in gold. The mosaics actually have most of the gold applied to the inside of the glass tesserae, so that the reflection of any light whatsoever might be refracted by a prism on each tiny piece of gold. The floor, now undulating like the lagoon itself is paved with rare and common marbles laid in the sixteenth century fashion. Like late cosmatesque pavements, the patterns remind one of rugs from the fabled east and especially from the main business partner of the Republic, the Empire whose main city, Orthodox or Muslim, was Constantinople. The walls are plain but rich marble, backdrop to the crowds of pilgrims.

The apsidal hemi-dome is dominated by a gigantic Christ Pantocrator, omnipresent, omniscient, omnipotent. It is central in position, monumental, demanding attention. The black-robed virgins orantes (praying while standing with arms outstretched, like a Hebrew priest) in each of the central domes preceding the sanctuary, are indicators, pointing to the divinity beyond all the theophanic, hierophanic, and kratophanic manifestations commemorated throughout the rest of the opulent church. They point to the Christ and to the sanctuary below Him.

In the days of the eastern liturgies in the space, the vast rood screen with the fourteen attendant saints beside the crucifix would have been less transparent than it is today. The pala d'oro, the golden panel with all the enamels of saints and all the precious jewels may actually have been a foil for the liturgy at one time. The pulpits, one on each side of the sanctuary but at least partly under the drum of the central dome, are vast platforms with precious porphyry walls, rather than dignified pulpits. They each sit on a single immense monolithic columnar base, two images of the axis mundi, across from one another. If one is good, two are better. Is this the Venetian motto?

This place obviously has influences other than the western liturgy. There is a stone presidential seat in the midst of stone choir benches lining the apse, like the banc at the basilica of St. Apollinaris in Ravenna. In the front of the clerical choir seats is a marble altar with a columned baldachino.

There are many side chapels with votive altars. One of these is a large baptistery on the south side of the nave. The floor plan is a Greek cross but the number of small places and bridges across architraves make the place seem to ramble in all directions. The darkness of the vast interior space is filled with little lights, glowing in reflection, from the mosaic facets. The lights are small and flickering like candle light except in the south transept where a tremendous flamboyant Gothic rose with frosted, leaded glass bathes the facets with so much light that the walls virtually beam rather than flicker. This quarter of the church seems more Bahnhoff than chiesa, more train station than church, because of this intrusion of light.

The atmospheric and archetypal "requirements" are all present in this place but the immensity of the pulpits, the monumentality of the rood screen and the golden panel at the altar, blocking the choir, make the view cluttered. The sound of tourists, rather than pilgrims, bounding off the hard surfaces makes for auditory noise which compounds the distractions of the visual noises.

I do not think that the images on the ceiling in all the domes and the arches are any more distracting than the ceiling of Gala Placidia.

Dupre describes the "new" cathedral in St. Louis, Missouri (pg. 113). She says that it is has the largest number of mosaics in one place on earth. The building is Byzantine and Romanesque. Like San Marco, it has a number of influences but, under the design program of Barnett, Haynes, and Barnett, there is an integrity to both the decoration and the overall unity or focus. There is a large white marble rood, or crucifixion group, making a significant shining indicator while affording a locus for the eyes to wander and prayerfully return to the eucharistic mystery on the altar, itself under a baldachino which adds to the sense of holy-of-holies in a grand space like this.

Dupre also speaks of the Metropolitan Cathedral in Managua, Nicaragua (pg. 142) making allusion to San Marco in Ricardo Legorreta's design. The large cube has a profusion of sixty-three domes ascending to a central pinnacle, looking somewhat like Hagia Sophia or the blue Mosque, somewhat like San Marco, and somewhat like the Templo Mayor at Teotihuacan, Mexico. It is a massive building in gray concrete with some large, strong color passages near the doors. The interior has four reinforced concrete piers, an interlinear structure of concrete coffers, made by intersecting beams. Some strong color is afforded by light and paint but there is no color on the apse where the sanctuary is. There are some seats and a large altar and a pulpit but basically the vast space is a "white box" the side chapels are outdone by the crystal cage in which an antique bloody crucifix is housed. The domed concrete chapel is perforated by a myriad of little lighted windows. This "side chapel" allows focus for meditation which the main space does not afford. Except during the liturgy, there is no reason to be in the large and lovely expanse of space. So it is a place but not really a space except during the rituals of eucharist, confirmation, marriage, or funeral. Outside of ritual or performance, only the most contemplative of minimalists would find God here.

Gothic Churches

Suger, Abbot of the Royal Abbey of St. Denis, took a shine to gothic arches. Rather, he gave a "shine" to Gothic arches. He fueled the first fires which filled Europe with a new order of magnitude in church engineering and ecclesiastical aesthetics. Apparently the crusades brought contact with the shape of the ancient arch at Ctesiphon and the Arab invention came into the west as a result of the questionable escapades that followed the call to arms issued by Bernard of Citeau and Pope Urban II at the Benedectine Abbey of Ste. Marie Madaleine in Vezeley in 1095. Like the preservation of the knowledge of the classical civilizations which Arabic culture preserved and developed for the reintroduction into western culture in the intellectual heartland of Moorish Spain, the Arab culture had developed an engineering capacity which allowed the nesting churches of Christendom to learn how to fly.

The arch allowed a number of possibilities. The flying buttress permitted vast walls of glass to take the place of stone in the clerestories of great building programs in cathedrals. The race which had started in the Romanesque Era with nobles, churchmen, monasteries, and pilgrimage cities vying to build the biggest and the best, produced great edifices, Laon, St. Michael in Hildesheim, St. Remy at Rheims, Autun, Speyer, Saint Sernin de Toulouse, Mont Saint Michel, San Isidro in Leon, Santiago de Compostela, Durham Cathedral, Tournai Cathedral, the great monastery at Cluny, and the baptistery, tower, and cathedral at Pisa., among them There are thousands of thousand-year-old churches. (For great pictures and fine commentary, see Rolf Toman ed., Achim Bednorz photographer, Romanesque: Architecture, Sculpture, Painting, Konemann 1997) Jungmann finds that the Romanesque monastic system developed a massive distance between clergy and people, the ritual and the congregation becoming more and more separate. He says:

> The line of separation between altar and people, between clergy and laity…was now made into a broad line of demarcation, not to say a wall of division. This had effect even on church architecture. The altar was moved back to the rear wall of the apse. In cathedrals, that necessitated transferring the bishop's throne; it is now generally placed at the side of the altar. (ibid. pg. 83)

Romanesque masterpieces, they were the base on which the Gothic Era built its delights. Delusions of grandeur led often enough to catastrophe but bigger and better would afford a couple of lifetimes of livelihood and prosperity for generations of workers on the project, artisans, masons, artists——and bakers, rope makers, carpenters, hunters, farmers. Whole civilizations arose around the building of the church fabric of Christendom. (For a good story about how this interdepence all came about see David Macaulay, Cathedral: The Story of Its Construction, Houghton Mifflin, 1978.) After the "Dark Ages" light!

The Debate

Two camps arose over the construction and outfitting of the house of God. The Cistercian reform of the Cluniac monastic system was joined by Bernard of Clairvaux, a man with a fine mind and a strong will. Louis Lekai says of him:

> After rebuking the Cluniacs for their intemperance in food and clothing, Bernard sharply criticized the luxury of their buildings, "..the soaring heights and extravagant lengths and unnecessary widths of the churches,...their expensive decorations and their novel images, which catch the attention of those who go to pray, and dry up their devotion." However, he carefully restricted his criticism to the monastic churches while admitting the significance of art elsewhere for the common people: "Bishops have a duty toward both wise and foolish. They have to make use of material ornamentation to rouse devotion in a carnal people, incapable of spiritual things. But we no longer belong to such people. (The Cistercians: Ideals and Reality, quoting the Apologia ad Guillelmun Abbatem, Kent State University Press, 1977, pg. 263)

Quoting the Abbot Suger, Irwin Panofsky gives a rationale which exonerates expensive taste in church building much more leniently:

> To me, I confess one thing has always seemed preeminently fitting: that every costlier or costliest thing should serve, first and foremost, for the administration of the Holy Eucharist. If golden pouring vessels, golden vials, golden little morters used to serve, by the word of God or the command of the Prophet, to collect

> the blood of goats or calves of the red heifer: how much more must golden vessels, precious stones, and whatever is most valued among all created things, be laid out, with continual reverence and full devotion, for the reception of the blood of Christ! Surely neither we nor our possessions suffice for this service. (Abbot Suger on the Abbey Church of St. Denis and its Art Treasures, Princeton University Press, 1946, 1973, pg. 65)

There are abbey churches of great simplicity and beauty built during the Middle Ages. The Benedictine Abbey churches of Pomposa, Assisi, and Vezelay; the Augustinian Abbey of Saint Remi in Reims; the Cistercian churches of Fontenay and Fossanova are all very bare, austere, in decoration. Their structures are built in the same architectural language as their Romanesque or Gothic neighbors, but the statements are different. These austere places often have no tribune, no triforium, and have spare decoration. Often only a Rood and one or a couple of statues, a single painting. They are not usually devoid of simplicity or of devotional aids. They are austere, spare in a kind of symmetrically balanced western Zen Buddhist karma consciousness.

There are modern churches which have this kind of austerity, with the attention to detail that makes them eminently focused and places where the pilgrim can learn and pray, in personal contemplation or in communal ritual prayer. The Dominican Chapelle du Rosaire, designed by Henri Mattisse for the Dominican Sisters at Vence, has that focus, as does the Louise Nevelson Chapel of the Good Shepherd at St. Peter's Lutheran Church in New York City (Dupre, pp. 120, 121), and St. Andrew's Anglican-Episcopal Church in Tokyo by Hisao Koyama Atelier (Takao Fujiki, trans. Hiroshi Watanabe, Religious Facilities: New Concepts in Architecture & Design, Meisei Publications 1997, pp. 24-30).

Hisao Koyama Atelier's Cistercian Abbey Church in Imari, Japan (ibid. pp, 58-63) has an austerity and a clarity of focus, similar to their St. Andrew's. There is an iconic focus in the flatter Japanese Anglican church, a large sculpture of the Risen Christ hovers over the altar. In the former, the convent chapel, a large and delicate crucifix hangs in the space before a proscenium arch wall. Under the arch stands the altar, between the place for the nuns and the place for the clergy. The tabernacle is centrally located on the back wall. There is a large wooden sculpture of the Virgin and

Child, very organic, in wood with feminine bulges which occupies the nave, to the right of the sanctuary. Otherwise the space is clear. There are six large simple peaked windows on the side walls. A light tower lets filtered light into the sanctuary, in a hidden way which would make le Corbusier know he'd had an influence.

A Little Chapel with the feel of a Gothic or Romanesque pilgrimage stop

Sr. Giotto Moots, O.P.'s Sagrada Chapel in Old Town Albuquerque, New Mexico, also has, in a very small space, a profound sense of the presence of mystery and the comfortable welcome that says, "sit, stay, pray by yourself or with us." The place has three chambers separated from one another by significant pieces of furniture. The pilgrim enters from a courtyard shared by a gallery of religious art, a restaurant of religious simplicity and a museum of the State of New Mexico. There are trees and shrubs. The pilgrim enters a small open-doored narthex whose wall opposite the entrance is graced by a framed collographic print of the Virgin of Guadaloupe. Before it, on a raised shelf of stuccoed half-wall lie votive candles. To the right is a holy water font, the water in a blue-glazed round bowl imbedded in a stupa in the center of a passageway. To the left is a liturgical calendar year in a painted plexiglass circular window. It fills the small chamber with its soft light. That mandala is constantly evident to everyone in the small chapel. It and the cross at the other end are the only minimal iconic presences. About such mandalas, Carl Jung says:

> The mandala is an archetypal image whose occurrence is attested throughout the ages. It signifies the wholeness of the self. The circular image represents the wholeness of the psychic ground or, to put it in mythic terms, the divinity incarnate in man. (C.G. Jung, Memories, Dreams, and Reflections, ed. Aniela Jaffe, Vintage Books 1965. Pg. 335)

As the pilgrim passes beyond the font s/he enters a small chamber with three rough hewn but polished seats on each side. There are only six seats, large with dark wood, words carved on the backs over the heads of any who would sit there. There is nothing of trite banner art in these carvings of words. They are profoundly simple. The wood of the chairs is placed on and imbedded into the stuccoed adobe. The simplicity is helped by a south western US painting of a tree of life on the floor and up the walls of this very small holy place.

At the far end of this small chamber is another portal. At its left is another pillar for the reading. In the center of the doorway is another, larger pillar; this is the altar. The chamber beyond this doorway is the sanctuary, its floor raised one step. There is a stuccoed place for the priest to sit. The back wall holds a rough hewn cross which seems to have a personality given it by the desert; so there is no corpus but one feels His presence just like one can while standing near a massive saguaro cactus. The ceiling is rough cut pine planks. So this place has the five necessary functional furnishings for eucharist. The presidential seat, the seats in the nave, the altar, the ambo, and the enclosure. The archetypes are on the floor with the tree of life claiming in southwest desert Indian way that this is a cosmic center. The tree is evident in the seats and ceiling, too. The sky is evident in the forecourt and in the clerestory. The water in the entry stupa. The earth is contiguous within and without. The profusion is profound but in only six massive (monumental) seats. The progressive entry is self evident. The whole place has a focus in the mandala and the cross. Even though there is no traditional iconic presence, that cross in this place has the power to evoke the presence. This is a powerful holy place!

The Madeleine

This church was built after the Carolingian and Ottonian "renovations." The court of Charlemagne had already developed a whole new way of looking at the Eucharist. The little round disk of unleavened bread was designed so that the "hostia," the host, could be exhibited. The impression that a raredos would be designed as a frame for a monstrance was soon to enliven the development of the altar table as platform, not only did this require that the mensa, table, be attached to the wall, it reinforced the idea that the altar was where the "Church Militant prayed to and through the Church Triumphant for the Church Suffering," the priest leading an army in prayer. The presence of the dead among the living came to be symbolized in the altar which held relics within. The image became more coffin than table. This paradigmatic image fit well with dead bodies incorrupt being displayed under the mensa itself. The cult of the worship of relics got joined to the liturgy of the Eucharist. The church as frame for the frame of the altar develops in the late Romanesque, grows to a universal conception during the Gothic, and becomes the norm during the Renaissance. After that the Council of Trent and the Missal of Pius V take it for granted that the altar faces the wall and the tabernacle sits in the middle of the retable, occasionally the whole sculptural conceit is fulfilled when the monstrance is "enthroned," or enshrined as the focal point of the whole church interior.

The pilgrim enters the nave of this abbey church through a tall narthex, the antechamber, whose high small windows give a gentle daylight to the empty room with a stone stairwell on the north wall. The door into the nave is split by a trumeau (the pier dividing the two doors and supporting the architrave) over which sits one of the most famous tympana (the panel of carving above the architrave within the arch) of Christendom. The twisted Christ, enthroned within a mandorla. The vesica piscis, which would be formed by the intersection of two circles is called a "mandorla" because of its almond shape; it is used throughout the Middle Ages as a sign for the presence of God. By extension it sometimes surrounds the Virgin Mary. The frame for the Virgin of Guadalupe, for instance, has the native woman painted on the tilma surrounded by rays in the form of a vesica piscis a kind of "fish frame," which elevates her status. This Christ is seated on an imperial throne, one of the usual images of the Christ in the first millennium (the others being the Last Supper, the Good Shepherd, and the Pantocrator). The Christ is, however, also in a half standing position with both legs together; He is in crucifixion pose.

This is truly a transition between two worlds, this portal into the Madeleine, because this Jesus is both ensconced on the throne of the first millennium wherein the Christ became the center of the Kingdom on Earth, the counterpart and/or fulfillment of the Roman Empire, and figured as the crucified high priest of the second millennium wherein His suffering in, with, for, and by His humanity on the cross becomes His claim on the hearts of women and men who also suffer. Jungmann says, "In the sculptures of the Romanesque period the crucified saviour continued at first by a faint radiance of the reigning Christ, which completely disappears only with the advent of the Gothic. The reigning Christ himself, the Maiestas Domini, is amongst the favourite subjects of Romanesque sculpture." (Pastoral Liturgy, pg. 6) Adams is of the opinion that the Christ of Romanesque Europe was a feudal, judging Lord of the Apocalypse while the Christ of Gothic Europe had ascended the cross to redeem wretched humankind. The stone tympanum establishes an ambiguous Lord for pilgrims of both persuasions.

> Vezelay is full of sculpture on the doors and capitals. But fascinating as it is, one forgets about it when one looks through the door at the architecture on the interior. It is so harmonious that surely St. Bernard, who preached the Second Crusade here must have felt it to be an expression of the Divine Law and an aid to worship and contemplation. (Clark, Civilization, pg. 44)

The interest in the Crucified perhaps has something to do with the barely noticeable but verifiable bend of the eastern choir and ambulatory, off axis and to the south. There is a charming story told, about the Cathedral of Laon, that the masons wanted to bend the head of the cross, of the Christ, toward Jerusalem, or down in submission to death, or, as another interpretation has it, toward their own hometown in benediction! (Andre Louis Pierre, Cathedrales de France: Arts-Techniques-Societe, Imprimeries Oberthuers, 1962, pg. 234)

Passing under the blessing Christ the pilgrim is greeted by an expanse of ordered stone and glass. A large, cavernous space is gently lighted by a softly- stained, leaded-glass clerestory without pictures. The oriented hall welcomes the visitor to this half-light but directs his or her attention eastward by means of alternating light and dark courses of local stone and by the leaping rhythm of Romanesque ogival archivolts. At the crossing are steps into the choir whose stalls face one another and run eastward in this Gothic chancel toward the sanctuary lighted by the rounded apsidal clerestory. Henry Adams says, "…the heavy round arch is like old cognac compared with the champagne of the pointed and fretted spire…" (Adams, pg.61) The focus of the entire building is thus directed toward this eastern sacred point without any interruption other than the relatively small and unobtrusive rood. There is separation of clerical and lay naves but the height of both and the resultant vast unified space above both is a factor of unification.

The necessity of keeping the view to the altar clear is interesting because Jungmann tells how this is the period of the development of the cult of the Eucharist. The people were reluctant to receive the sacred species but believed that seeing the elevated host and later the host and chalice brought merit. It is here that the cult, still young, has not reached its most elaborate manifestations. Jungmann recalls the practice of side-altar masses begun in the ninth century (Missarum Solemnia Vol I, pg. 223), the establishment of nonpublic masses in the monasteries with large choirs and very small naves (ibid. pg. 206), the commemorative reception of the sacrament by nuns (Missarum Solemnia Vol. II pg. 365), and such reverential rationales as this by Peter of Blois (d. 1204): "...from frequent celebrations a low esteem is sure to develop, but from the infrequent celebration grows reverence for the sacrament." (ibid., pg.364) This church has, as its focus, the Lord, under whose benediction the pilgrim enters and at whose altar s/he stops. But the importance of the monkish community is such that even now, centuries after the last resident choir, the empty stalls still evoke a sense of their presence. The position of the monkish community is of great importance in the lineup of "powers" in the Church.

It is Jungmann's impression that until Thomas the worshiping Church was seen as the Bride at the Eucharist who offered the sacrifice of Christ, the High Priest. Then in Thomas' scholastic followers' teachings against heresy,

> ...the Church's action was now seen not under the aspect of grace and the Holy Spirit common to all the faithful but under the aspect of the powers inherent in the Church, the powers, namely, that are conferred upon chosen members of the Church by Christ himself. Since (it was reasoned) the priest alone can consecrate, the participation and action of the faithful become insignificant under this new orientation. (The Mass, pg. 124)

In another place he tells us that by the Gothic period:

> The Mass is viewed almost exclusively as an action of God. The priest alone is active. The faithful, viewing what he is performing, are like spectators looking on at a mystery-filled drama of our Lord's way of the cross.... The eucharistia has become an epiphania.
> (Missarum Solemnia Vol I, pg. 117)

Vast crowds of pilgrims and crusaders, stopping at St. Mary Magdalen, heard God's Word proclaimed here. As in other churches of Europe in these centuries, a new element –the pulpit—became a fixed part of the architecture. The pulpit here is a raised platform placed for maximum visibility and audibility. This simple pulpit at Vezelay is placed well outside the sanctuary and even well beyond the precincts of the monks. The pulpit is for the laity to hear the word proclaimed and, even more, to hear the educated clergyman's exhortations. The Eucharistic Liturgy itself is far away, though still visible. The pilgrim community gathers to sing and to listen, perhaps to pray but the liturgy is way off in the distance. This is the period Jungmann tells of, the time when the people needed to be exhorted to receive communion at least yearly. The aura of the sacred had been almost totally distanced from the profane. The inhabitants of the terrible century described by Barbara Tuchmann are the original pilgrims who prayed here.

So there is a pulpit. There are many thrones for the holy monks; the abbott's is portable or, like the stalls of the monks, to the side of the choir—even he should take a deferential position before the mysterium. The altar is a large marble affair from the late Gothic period, but its predecessor was also in this spot of the easternmost, interior focus, inaccessible and actually cordoned off from the ambulatory by a carved choir screen. Jungmann says:

> ...in the early Middle Ages a new movement set in, which gradually moved the altar into the background in the rear of the choir. This is but the architectonic expression of an intellectual movement which stressed more and more the sacredness and aloofness of the mystery and restricted immediate access to it to the clergy. (Missarum Solemnia Vol. I, pg.256)

The enclosure is, however, for all; the domus is a round, arched barrel-vault which becomes more pointed as it approaches the sanctuary. But the mysterium, the monks, and the pilgrims are housed in the same space. The nave is adequately large for vast pilgrim crowds but uncluttered so that the attention can remain constantly eastward.

This church is still quite appropriate for large liturgical celebrations with the panoply of processions and vast crowds. Its sense of mystery is intact even with its great wealth of art's products. Even were a small community to choose to celebrate within the choir of the sanctuary, they could share in an intimate celebration uninterrupted by these "products" intruding on the space because of the very focus of the entire structure; here beauty can remain in the service of the community subject only to the knowledgeable use of the treasure.

The atmosphere is very quiet due to the soft stone and the many recesses in the arcade and in the tribune. The light is very soft as so often in the churches built of limestone or marble and with large glazed portions. A half-light filters through translucent but not transparent windows. There is plenty of free space above the heads of the assemblies, clerical or lay; a sense of uncluttered emptiness invites the spirit. The thickness of the walls and the height of the roof and the profusion of the columns make one aware of the monumental presence of this church.

The archetype of stone is everywhere, in the floors, pillars, walls, and ceiling. The tree stands at first entrance symbolically in the pillar in the trumeau (an axis mundi); the symbol is also in the very wood of the choir stalls and the pulpit. Water seems not to be present in the symbols other than in the little fonts. The sky is just beyond, celebrated in tracery frames around the thousands of rondels of pastel glass. The floor of stone spreads an earthiness about in its color and smoothness. The sanctuary seeming at ultimate remove from the holy narthex beyond which is the holier nave, beyond which is the choir, holier still. This progression is a fine example of Eliade's mountain-city-temple.Other examples of such serene space are plentiful. Laon's massive cathedral, the last of the old Carolingian kingdom's centers, was built like Vezelay at the crossroads between the eras. It was to have seven towers. It actually does have five. It is famous for the twice- or thrice- life size beasts of burden, donkeys, oxen, to commemorate their work in the building of the "city of God." This cathedral commands a spectacular site at the top of a mountain in the center of a once flourishing city. Even today one can climb from the train station straight skyward up thousands of steps to the pinnacle where the cathedral stands (or one can ride a funicular). The restored cruciform white marble building with a crossing tower lantern, under which the modern French have place their sanctuary with portable refectory table as altar, portable iron pulpit as ambo, and portable Louis XV chairs as the cathedrae, the presidential seats. The nave extends in three directions. The choir is cordoned off by an old iron rood screen. The walls of the enclosure are pierced by restored cobalt rondels in the terminal walls of each arm of the cross. There are also seven lancets under the eastern rondel. The whole place glows a heavenly blue, reflected off Baroque marble screens at the bottom of each of the arcade bays. This place is spectacular as space, too. Like Vezelay it seems timeless and protected by vast coffers of governmental funds.

St. John's Abbey and St. Louis Priory: American Benedictines Making

Authentic Simple Spaces Work like the vast Priories of their Illustrious Past

There are other examples of such space as Vezelay or Laon, bathed in serenity, born in "interesting times." According to the old Chinese curse interesting times create waters difficult to navigate. In our era, Marcel Breuer's St. John's Abbey Church in Collegeville Minnesota, is built in the modern idiom of concrete and space. Breuer was Bauhaus-trained and sought the simple in his ideals of design.

Roger Kennedy in American Churches (Stewart, Tabori & Chang, Publishers, 1982, pp 61-63) speaks of both St. John's and St. Louis. Of St. John's he says:

> Breuer's church places the altar at the center, surrounded by seating for 1,600. The members of the monastic community, including the teachers of the school and the university, are seated around one segment of the circle, the townspeople and the students around the other segments, leaving space for the choir—itself split in two parts to provide for antiphonal singing of Benedictine plainsong. This coming together around the common liturgical center, for the central unifying liturgy In which all participate, the looking across the Sacrament to the other participants, unites clergy and laity, teacher and student…
>
> …The primary liturgical elements are ordered in the sequence in which they are experienced in the life of a Roman Catholic—baptismal font, church door, confessionals, Communion tables, and altar, along the central axis of the building. Someone, perhaps Breuer, perhaps one of the congregation led by Abbot Baldwin Dworschak, conceived of the whole space as being like a bell…as if to enlarge the sound of prayer, of songs of praise."

The arrangement of all the furniture, the procesional arrangement of liturgical functions, and the explanations given by Kennedy all indicate that this building is profoundly considered, an intellectual as well as an aesthetic achievement.

> Dom Columba Cary-Elwes, former prior of the Saint Louis Priory in Saint Louis, Missouri, once spoke of the relationship of

theological tradition and innovation:

> Strange as it may seem, the very fact that the Benedictine spirit is so deep in tradition made it unlikely that any of these expressions of the past would be the expression of the present-day members.... Tradition in theology is not sticking to the letter of a primitive text, but rather an intrinsic growth, a repeated restatement in new terms, intelligible to each age. So, too, in architecture, tradition is not static but living....

> The atmosphere of the interior of the church is one of light, visibility, and serenity, though only 6 percent of the walls are of glass. Light, which also comes from the skylight, is central to the monks' and architects' program. They wished to create a space of maximum visibility for all participants to encourage "participating, not watching." The altar is encircled by seating for the congregation, originally to be largely schoolboys and monks, now serving a parish community of five hundred as well. Only six pews separate the furthermost seat from the sanctuary, gathering "all into a central unity."

Like Laon and Vezelay, St. John's and St. Louis are remarkably empty of iconic references. How is it that this thread is so noticeable in the tapestry of twentieth century church architecture. Is it really true that in an era when most can read, there is really not any reason to celebrate mysteries in stone and paint? Is it simply a mark of our era that the austere and empty space best offers the range of possibilities that people need in God? Do we all need to dissociate from images of a human, male Godhead with power and holiness? Do we need to drop the appealing devotion to the tender and powerful human female who mothered and nurtured God in her home?

It is significant that places which are mostly museum are devoid of tabernacles in their larger liturgical spaces. It would seem that church buildings are only to be used as they function for ritual prayer. They are not to teach the gospel or doctrine or dogma unless someone is talking or reading. These places are not to be used for private meditation because they are only stage sets for ritual prayer. This seems to be the modern reductionist concept.

I think that with the Benedictine penchant for austerely empty, modern masterpieces of architecture, it might be well to revisit the thought of Bernard of Clairvaux. He said that there might be reason for bishops to consider the needs of the people to learn about the Church and be drawn to the Church by masterpieces of visual arts in glass, sculpture, painting, and even vessels, while we, the monkish class, are no longer part of that needy human community. Perhaps, there is still reason to provide the sustenance afforded by the artistic expression of believers who do not produce prayer only in words or silence.

Does this idea, that there should be no art in the presence of the holy-of-holies, have a basis in the beginning of the modern era? As we look at the buildings built for later generations, the Renaissance, the Baroque-counter-reformation, the revival periods (Greek, Neo classical, Beaux Arts, Gothic and Romanesque Revivals), let us be aware that the role of images changes with the self- awareness of the people. As we consider Art Nouveau, Art Deco, Arts and Crafts, Queen Victoria, Queen Anne, Art Moderne, Bauhaus, Post Modern as the principles behind our buildings, let us think of the future as being born in the present. What do images mean for our own era?

The Cathedral of the Assumption in Burgos

Once the influence of a great successful cathedral was felt in the Gothic Era, there were contenders for surpassing it. Suger at St. Denis introduced the arch. Then the windows got bigger and better. The flying buttress led to more vast walls of glass. The blue of Chartres' windows led to lots of dark blue clerestories. The height of Köln, the depth of Sevilla, the breadth of Milano, the length of Amiens, the height of the crossing at Wells or Salisbury and Beauvais —each achievement meant pilgrims in the crypts, commerce in the streets, money in the coffers. The race was on and cities vied to outdo one another.

The beautiful five-aisled blue heaven of St. Etienne in Bourges led, on the other side of the Pyrenees to the vast building campaign which has given us the Cathedral of the Assumption in Burgos. There were other places to compete with within the Iberian Peninsula. Santiago de Compostela had the pilgrims. Sevilla had the beauty. Leon had los Reyes Catolicos. Burgos would have everything. Robert Branner implies that the daughter is too free at this point, a "contamination" rather than an "evolution." (Robert Branner, La Cathedrale de Bourges et sa Place dans l'Architecture Gothique, Editions Tardy, 1962, pp 172-175)

The visitor enters the Westwerk, the west front, under the pedimented (Renaissance or Baroque) tympanum, and is immediately confronted by the walls of the choir. The pillars are massive, laid stone on stone but seeming monolithic; they are carved deep with folds and figures. The walls of the choir which must be circumambulated are also covered with bas reliefs of salvation history. There are chapels all along the sides of the nave; some are immense like the first on the south which holds the "Christ of Burgos." A little corpus with real skin, eyelashes, glass eyes, teeth, it is the size of a house cat on a cross. The fluorescent lights were probably not there when St. Teresa de Avila, great doctor of the Church, reformer of the Carmelites, and leader among the Spanish mystics of her era, felt a great devotion welling up in response to the crucifix in the cathedral. But there it is, a devotional tour de force.

The chapel of Sta. Tecla and that of Sant'Anna are crowded beyond comprehension with polychromed wooden statues. The raredos of the Sant'Anna altar has the Tree of Jesse as its theme. In the chevet the radiating chapels are guarded by great wrought iron or bronze gates. The principal eastern chapel of the constables Don Pedro Fernandez de Velasco and his wife Doña Mencia de Mendoza is a memorial whose main feature is their tomb laid at the foot of the altar facing the east wall. Above there is a starburst lantern of stone tracery and glass; it repeats a larger one over the crossing.

The choir fills the western nave completely and ends opening onto the crossing beyond which is the sanctuary. The misericordes of the choir are late, carved dark wood. There are a couple of ancient stands for the very large books of hours that would be used by the monks together (This is before the printing press would allow them each to have his own copy of the chant and the words). The building within the building is among the most imposing in Spain but there are many "museum-quality" cathedrals, chock full of monastic furniture which was necessary in the days of the canons and monks who would fill them regularly to pray for the rest of the Church. Now they are "curiosities" as liturgical furniture but, as here in Burgos, so beautiful that they are hard to consider removing.

The crossing is an empty space, full of Persian rugs and chairs but empty of permanent furniture. It is lighted by the rather extraordinary lantern, another starburst of Gothic tracery and glass, reaching up, far up into the pinnacle of the crossing. The sanctuary, beyond the crossing toward the east, is shielded from the ambulatory by deeply carved stone screens. Those parts of this interior building composed of the choir and sanctuary which could be penetrated are covered by intricate iron and bronze grates reaching twenty feet into the space above, the space capped by the magnificent lantern.

This cathedral is one which, over the years, has been so plenteously endowed that the space has been filled. The mysterium all but edged out. Indeed, John Allyne Gade caricatures the place with these words, "Burgos seems much more emotional than sensitive. Riotous excess and empty display take the place of restrained and appropriate decoration." (Cathedrals of Spain, Houghton Mifflin, 1911, pp. 39, 40)

In The Dynamics of Architectural Form, Rudolph Arnheim says that people are not aesthetically displeased so much by the lack of order as by the "clash of uncoordinated orders" (University of California Press, 1977, pg. 163)). This Burgos is an example of what Arnheim calls "The clash of uncoordinated orders."

Problem Places:

Canterbury, Wells, Westminster Abbey, St. Denis, The Churches of the Frari and San Zanipoli in Venice

There are other Gothic places where history has so imposed on the space that there can be no accommodation to the present. For instance there was an historical difficulty in the very foundation of the cathedral at Wells. The tower, needing reinforcement, had to be preserved from collapse. The solution was uniquely ingenious. The inverted arch on top of the arch which continues the arcade across the front of the "nave" is repeated on the four sides of the crossing forming a small, dark room in the very center of the church. The rather vast nave, now lighted very much by plain glass windows is a hall with an altar at its front and with a pulpit to the side. There are also some small chapels in the front of the nave, between the first piers of the arcade—a little building really, completely enclosed, playful but very distracting. The chevet is vaulted in a much later Gothic tracery, much more ornate than the vaulting of the nave and of the transepts. The choir is, therefore, of an almost completely different century in its very skin; its union with the earlier nave is impossible to both physical and intellectual appreciation. The small room beneath the crossing is only a passageway between the large halls, hardly the central spot at the center of the world. The individual chambers, the arms of the cross in plan, might very each be a wonderful place for liturgy, but the whole divided cathedral speaks volumes about the compartmentalization that history sometimes imposes on peoples. Like the Jerusalem Cross, this, at first stupendously appealing monument of the ONE Church, is actually a symbol of the divided and segregated parts!

Canterbury and Westminster Abbey are similarly overladen with their history. The tombs and monuments in each place so fill the consciousness of the visitor that s/he cannot ignore them with anything less than a monumental effort. Their problem is a superabundance of tomb monuments. Similar repositories exist all over the world. The good idea of the Catacomb or the Gala Placidia tomb, run amuck by too much commemoration and competitive commemoration at that! Consider all the monuments in St. Denis, all the notables in the Franciscan and Dominican churches in Venice, Florence, Rome as musea of monuments, quite enjoyable for a tour but not a place where it is easy to pray without distraction either in ritual or private prayer.

Of Westminster Abbey Lethaby says two things which both indicate the importance of the place as sacred to the memory of art and as too full for liturgy to be easily conducted there. In the former instance he writes:

> From its crowded associations, and the many lovely minor works it contains,…this church must be held by Englishmen as the supreme work of art in the world. (Westminster Abbey and the King's Craftsmen: A Study of Mediaeval Building, EPDutton, 1906, pg. 8)

In the instance of this place and its appropriateness for the liturgy, he indicates his own feeling that it is too cluttered with these words:

> The Church within has been little injured, except by the erection of pompous tomb-trophies, and modern sham Gothic fittings and glass, which are even more injurious because specious and confusing. (ibid. pg. 3)

Across the river in Burgos

While in Burgos we can see a church within the yearning view of the cathedral's south portal. The Carmelite Church designed by Pedro Rodriguez had two iconic necessities to deal with. The corner property is filled by the ziggurat steps which afford a stained-glass mountain climbing into the cityscape from the river. The visitor is aware of the glass mountain into which s/he has entered only after having descended down the ramp of the floor toward the sanctuary and turned around to leave. So one comes in from the river front, blesses him or herself with water at the door, enters this chamber which has a massive blond wood sculpture of the Christ. It has noticeable seams and so has been glued together of many parts. The color is a warm but natural wood color. The image is an articulate figure of the corpus of Christ with realistic wounds, particularly noticeable at the knees. The sculpture is demanding but not grotesque. It points to the sanctuary but, because of the color and the massive size, can be ignored in order to pray. This is quite a significant iconic presence. There is also a statue of the Virgin of Mount Carmel, smaller than life, colored somewhat realistically, completely unavoidable on the wall right below the crucifix and too near the altar.

This little jewel box of a church has a gritty feel but it is very accessible to the modern pilgrim, other worldly because of the grim Christ, full of promise because of the color, an axis mundi, a cosmic pillar whose power shoots up from the table of sacrifice and down below into the earth, the descent felt by the pilgrim as s/he enters the church. This place is of a time but it has a power focused in the preaching of that great artwork which invites meditation, but which also indicates where the congregant should place his or her attention, right there in the scriptures at His feet, right there on the table where the sacred species will give life to the Lord whose image this is.

The presence of the Carmen Christ in other old cathedrals?

The Catholic Cathedral of Westminster just down the street from the Abbey has a Byzantine Revival silhouette. The Cathedral Basilica of the Immaculate Conception in Washington DC mimics it. The English cathedral, however, is very dark inside. With striped polychromy in its walls., it is reminiscent of German Romanesque churches, like Hildesheim, or French like Vezelay, or Italian like Pisa, Siena, and Orvieto. There is a simplicity to the big space. There is, however, a commanding focus in the immense red rood which hangs over the sanctuary, doing, in the big dark English cathedral, what the yellow wooden corpus does in the small Spanish church. The cluttered monument which is Santa Croce in Florence had for centuries a polychromy crucifix by Cimabue. After that massive and memorable focus was destroyed in the flood of 1966, the leaders of church and state saw fit to find a similar treasure from the School of Giotto to replace it.

So there is some lesson to learn here. It is possible to have a focus in a large place or a small place afforded by a rood. The delicate balance between helpful reminder and intrusive barrier is where the designer of the church space should set his or her sights. The iconic image should be capable of supporting the visitor who wishes to make contemplative contact. It should also be capable of slipping into the background during the Eucharistic Liturgy so that the congregant might pray with the universal community. It should also aid in keeping the congregant attentive to the reading of the sacred scriptures or listening to the homily of the priest.

The presence of such an iconic image within the sanctuary, contrary to an opinion popular in recent days, if chosen well and placed correctly, will not be a distraction. It is the evidence of two millennia that Catholics pray well with images which aid the imagination. Those who protest have been, in the history of the Catholic Church, relegated to the outer darkness. Puritanism, Quakerism, Quietism, Calvinism, Iconoclasm have all had good reform points to make but, in the end, each has been found wanting or found itself wanting what the universal Church could not or would not deliver. And so, we suffered a dismemberment.

Can it be, on the other hand, that in the present dispensation we have finally gotten it right. Finally we are willing to have no art in the sanctuary because we, like all the reform movements in the past, have arrived at that pristine and serene moment in the faith of a people wherein there is such clarity that imagination and yearning for anything OTHER, anything "mysterious," in the here and now, is not only unnecessary but impertinent? I think my answer to each of these questions is an indefatigable NO. Perhaps the reader will have reached another conclusion by the end of this reading. Perhaps all the reforms of the Age of Enlightenment were so right that now the Roman Church reaches a timely rapprochment.

Chapter Five: Renaissance

A New World

The result of Luther's refusal to abide by the selling of indulgences to foster the building of the Church (especially the new papal basilica under Leo X, Giovanni de Medici who had said supposedly, "God has seen fit to give us the papacy. It is our intention to enjoy it.") has wide reverberations. Jungmann tells us:

> The was felt even in sections of Europe which remained staunchly Catholic, so that as early as 1528 we are told that in the church of Salzburg a hundred gratiani (priests who lived on stipends) could formerly be maintained more easily than now even a single one. (Missarum Solemnia, Vol I, pg. 132)
>
> After fifteen hundred years of unbroken development in the Rite of the Roman Mass, after the rushing and the streaming from every height and out of every valley, the Missal of Pius V was indeed a powerful dam holding back the waters or permitting them to flow through only in firm, well-built canals. At one blow all arbitrary meandering to one side or another was cut off, all floods prevented, and a safe, regular and useful flow assured. But the price paid was this, that the beautiful river valley now lay barren and the forces of further evolution were often channeled into the narrow bed of a very inadequate devotional life instead of gathering strength for new forms of liturgical expression. (ibid. pp 140 f)

Jungmann is sounding a lot like Archbishop Rembert Weakland speaking of what he sees as the danger from the "restorationists" who would, in his view, return us to the Church of the Renaissance, Baroque, and Romantic past which they prize:

> ..the restorationists hold to the position that the origins of the liturgical movement are to be found in Germany in the 1930's thereby diminishing the importance of the work of scholars in other countries like Belgium, England, France, or the United States itself. Perhaps they see then in the liturgical movement and its

> emphasis on the prominent role of the laity a reference to the Volksideologie of the Third Reich. (James Carroll in Constantine's Sword, borrowing from these restorationist sources, makes this explicit connection, even going so far as to relate—in an extremely bizarre way—this Nazi Volksideologie to the American "folk Masses" after Vatican II!)
>
> Whatever the source of the omission of any clear theology of the People of God in the liturgy, the restorationists are allergic to it. They freely accentuate the hierarchical nature of the liturgy as a mirror of the hierarchical nature of the church itself but subordinate the role of the people to their pre-Vatican II liturgical position. This way of de-emphasizing the role of the People of God assembled spills over into architecture as well. ("The Liturgy as Battlefield: What do 'restorationists' want?" Commonweal, 11 January 2002, pg. 13)

So the wheel turns and "there is nothing new under the sun," my son! (Ecclesiastes 1:9). The remark makes sense again, because the conflict has been going on about who should have power over what everybody else does since time began. Both Jungmann and Weakland seem to think that the liturgy itself has the protection of Something much greater than those who seek cultural control in order to protect it from change…

The Renaissance

The development of banking and marketing along with the "age of discovery" encouraged a renewed interest in the inheritances of Empire, the deposit of Greek culture, and the seeds of Christianity. Long forgotten but newly rediscovered, the seeds of classical culture, both philosophy and literature, awaken a humanistic approach to the reality of urban life. Renascimento, Renascence, Renaissance, there was a new awakening all over the old world to its past glories and an excitement about the possibilities of the new. Cathay and Tenochtitlan give a romance to a world too long in the dark, perhaps; their fabled riches calling forth revived dreams of glory in the common person.

Painters and sculptors interested anew in what they perceived as a classical ability particularly with anatomy, their heritage, engaged in pushing the edges of old restraints, the bonds of doing things in ways tried and true. Patrons endorsed bronze casting. Fresco allowed wall treatments far more ambitious than mural painting (and with far greater freedom than mosaic could permit). Oil painting liberated all the arts from the tyranny of solid architecture. Dance, theater, music, preaching had a more portable visual aid. Like stained glass in the Gothic era, painting brought a new paedagogy into the fore.

In architecture, the Pantheon offered something that hadn't been done in centuries. In the race to become the new Rome, the major cities of Italy were trying to create their own new backdrop so that Orvieto, Bologna, Siena, Milano, Napoli, Venezia, or Firenze could claim the inheritance of the firstborn. Florence already had a cathedral designed by Arnolfo di Cambio who had been mastermason of Santa Croce and a few other places within the city blessed by the good banking of Cosimo di Medici and his family. This family, perhaps destined to command much of European politics in one way or another over the next couple of centuries, had at the beginning of the Renaissance, pretensions of grandeur quite in competition with so many other families. They were also patrons of the arts. Their parish church, San Lorenzo, became a place for their patronage. The old sacristy there was designed by Filippo Brunelleschi, the new one by Michelangelo Buonarroti.

The octogonal baptistery in Florence was already ancient when the millennium began. It was subject to constant enrichment but it seemed inadequate as the main church of a city with such potential. So the cathedral was begun. That, too, seemed eventually inadequate, when it had to compete with the duomi of Siena, Orvieto, and Pisa. So, the race demanded a new program of civic building with new ideas, new engineering, and a thirst for the grand scheme. Filippo Brunelleschi found a way to understand the Pantheon. He discovered and/or invented ways to get a dome over a large open space without hindrance of great weight so that the interior could still have relatively large areas of glass. The dome was doubled with an inner dome supporting an outer one which in turn held up the inner one in precarious balance until the marvel could be stabilized both in fact and in the mind of the people of the city.

The Duomo of Florence, the Cathedral of Saint Mary of the Flowers, became a whole world and it invited competition which resulted in the domed church as a different structure on the horizon of cities of Christendom. The dome developed, in a metaphor of Brunelleschi's structure as a way to look at the relationship of the Church with God. The mysterium tremendum et fascinans, the mystery which both repels and attracts, both appealing and terrifying, is symbolized in a dome doubly hung over the square earth. The perfect geometric forms of square and circle, depicting since Pythagoras, the realms of earth and sky respectively, and metamorphosed in the Gothic Era into the rose window within a square frame, came into the Renaissance as a three dimensional structure which praises God and forms the people.

The funny thing about the fortuitous arrival of the dome in the western world at this time is that it fits so well as the hovering image for a new humanism. Right along with the painting and sculpture, the building celebrates God as man. Jesus comes off the throne of Empire, down from the cross of triumph, and enters into the imagination in stories, depicted in stone, paint, dance, opera, music. All in due course, the world of the heavenly kingdom becomes a dream for a reality on earth. The Renaissance brings back the Roman ideal of what a city should be, how a republic of ideas can become a reality.

Michelangelo's star rose soon after Brunelleschi's and he was commissioned to design a new plan for the papal church in Rome. Of course, the Bramante plan which Michelangelo adapted into non-existence was only the beginning of a long line of master masons' revisions on the papal powerhouse which was to be this great basilica. Michelangelo took succor at the Florentine breast. His poem declares his affection:

> Io faro la sorella,
> Gia piu gran, ma non piu bella.
>
> I will build her sister
> Bigger, yes, but not more beautiful.
> (Mary McCarthy, The Stones of Florence,
> Harcourt Brace, 1962, pg. 71)

His design was followed within a century by Sir Christpher Wren's St. Paul's in London, and then Czar Alexander I wanted one in St. Petersburg. The St. Isaac's, completed in 1857 according to plans of Auguste Ricard de Montferrand, became the fourth of the major domes of the modern world. Again czarist Russia, during the reigns of Victoria and Pius IX, Pio Nonno, seems to claim for the imperial capital significant congruence with the other major political influences in the modern world.

Of these four great domes, two have a central interior sanctuary just under the dome itself (St. Peter's and St. Mary's), all have a long nave making a latin cross in plan, and two have an eastern focus (St. Paul's and St. Isaac's). They are all very impressive as spaces and have been fine places for massive public liturgies, some televised with great visual success. The iconostasis in St, Isaac's, however, though cutting off the sanctuary and choir from the nave, is actually so massive that when its royal doors are open revealing the stained glass of the Resurrected Christ, between the massive mosaics of Jesus and the Mother of God, the whole place is focused on the altar and the priest who would read from the scriptures at the center of the iconostasis. The whole nave and holy-of-holies bathed in the soft light of the immense hovering dome, so high as to seem to cover the whole space of the whole cathedral. This focus and this image are strangely in the only one of those four major domes which is always only a state museum. Contemplation and learning are more than possible in this place. The ritual can only be experienced with doors closed. But larger than those closed royal doors would be needed to keep the experience of the place as space from the pilgrim!

Domes on cityscapes permeate the modern horizon as political powers perceive their need to penetrate the horizon with the breast of the nurturing earth, offering God, almost, human sustenance. Like the Egyptians or Hindus or Aztecs trying to marry Father Sky to Mother Earth, Karlskirk, Les Invalides, the Pantheon, St. Peter's, St. Paul's, St. Isaac's, Sacre Coeur, the Cathedral Basilica of the Immaculate Conception in D.C., and the Queen of Peace in Togo, Africa praise God, while giving continual homage to the achievement of Brunelleschi.

Renaissance Principles

The Renaissance saw the rebirth of many different strains of artistic purpose in Europe. Commerce and mercantile politics, exploration and imperial conquest, the growth of mystical prayer and human-centered religion were all old but new-again classical ideas, tremendous energy needing ordered, vivifying control.

The liturgy had become a communal ritual no longer; private votive masses could be said for the intentions of the Church (or its paying members) without the actual participation of the assembly, since the fourth century. Religious humility of the day so acknowledged divine activity and so de-emphasized the personal response to redemption that religious orders were hell-bent on encouraging mere attendance at liturgy, even of their membership, without suggesting reception of the Eucharist.

The renewal of the Church was part of the Renaissance; a reform movement based on the mystical and religious experiences of the saints was countered by a reform movement based on logic and intelligent investigations of the scriptures and documents of the Church's past. Leaders like Luther, Zwingli, and Calvin moved in one direction away from imagination to an analytical sense of restraint. Others, like Ignatius of Loyola, Theresa of Avila, Francis de Sales, and John of the Cross, ecouraged using the faculty of imagination as a foundation for contemplation. This dichotomy was alive throughout the Renaissance until the Council of Trent took sides. One movement in the Church was thus toward classical order, the other toward imaginative romance. Both were born in the Renaissance. They were solidified into camps in the following period, called the Reformation and Counter-Reformation or the Baroque Period. Germain Bazin borrows from Wolfflin to describe these very contemporary movements in art:

> Classical art does not turn its back on nature—it is an art of observation, but its aim is to go beyond the disorder of appearances and to seek that deeper truth which is the underlying order of the world. Classical compositions are simple and clear, each constituent part retaining its independence; they have a static quality and are enclosed within boundaries. The Baroque artist, in contrast, longs to enter into the multiplicity of phenomena, into the flux of things in their perpetual becoming—his compositions are dynamic and open and tend to expand outside their boundaries; the forms that go to make them are associated in a single organic action and cannot be isolated from each other. The Baroque artist's instinct for escape drives him to prefer "forms that take flight" to those that are static and dense; his liking for pathos leads him to depict sufferings and feelings, life and death at their

> extremes of violence, while the Classical artist aspires to show the human figure in the full possession of its powers. (Baroque and Rococo, trans. Jonothan Griffin, Oxford University Press, 1964, pp. 6,7)

In the liturgical life of the Church there is also this two-fold tendency. The artistic demand for order and simplicity resulted in the general rubrics of the Roman Mass being regularized for the known world in the Missal of Pius V, the result of the Council of Trent, but the other tendency had an outlet in the building of the Renaissance environment for liturgy. So, in Bazin's image of the continual swing of the pendulum from the classical to the baroque, the one follows the other as Hegel's thesis/antithesis/ synthesis, in a constant historical motion. In light of this insight, the Council of Trent and the subsequent Missale Romanum were the result of a classicizing tendency , and so a product of the Renaissance. Whereas, the Baroque building boom was born in a logically, as well as historically, later movement, antithetical almost to the doctrinal documents on which it was based.

The Pazzi Chapel

The hope for a classical rebirth is epitomized in the Pazzi Chapel, Brunelleschi's masterpiece in the cloister at Santa Croce. This is the quintessential Rainassance space, un fixed by more modern needs. Mary McCarthy again:

> The interior is a simple rectangle with four high narrow windows and bare white walls and a small apse. In the four corners tall closed arches are drawn in pietra serena on the white walls, like the memory of windows. Fluted pilasters with Corinthian capitals, also in pietra serena, are spaced along the bare walls, marking the points of support, and in the same way, the lunettes and supporting arches of the chapel are outlined in dark ribbons of stone rosettes enclosed in rectangles drawn on the white background. Arch repeats arch; curve repeats curve; rosette repeats rosette. The rectangles of the lower section are topped by the semi-circles of the lunettes and arches, which, in turn, are topped by the hemisphere of the cupola. The continual play of the basic forms and their variations—of square against round, deep against flat—is

> like the greatest music: the music of the universe heard in a small space.
>
> The twelve Apostles, by Luca della Robbia in dark-blue-and-white roundels, framed in pietra serena, are seated about the walls, just below a frieze of cherubs' heads and lambs, in the apse are wonderful immense gray scallop shells, and in the pendentives of the room itself, outranking the Apostles, sit the four Evangelists, cast in glazed terracotta by Luca della Robbia on Brunelleschi's designs, each with his attendant symbol and companion: Saint Luke with the Bull, Saint Mark with the Lion, Saint John with the Bird, and Saint Matthew with the Angel in the form of a Man. The colors of the terracotta glazes are clear and intensely beautiful in the severe gray-and-white room. The Bird is raven-black, the Lion chocolate, the Bull brown; the robes of the Evangelists are glittering, glassy white or yellow or translucent green; and these four great Teachers with their books are placed in wavy blue backgrounds, as though they were sitting comfortably at the bottom of the sea. The chapel is not large but seems to hold the four corners of the earth and all the winds securely in its binding of pietra serena. In the blue cupoletta, above the little apse, with its plain altar, like a table, there is a Creation of Man and the Animals. No more exquisite microcosm than the Pazzi Chapel could be imagined, for everything is here, in just proportion and in order, as the Seventh Day of Creation, when God rested from His labors, having found them good. (op.cit. pg. 73)

This description, gives what would seem a perfect example of the perfect Renaissance space for the Eucharist. The apse separates the sacrament and the clergy form the nave by a couple of steps. For the modern Eucharist, there would have to be brought in an ambo for the scripture reading, and a seat for the presider. If these were appropriately plain and in pietra serena like the walls, terracotta like the rondels, wood like the doors, or even marble like the altar, the whole would seem appropriate for today's liturgy. The entrance across a monastery garden, through the triumphal arched portico and into the little, obviously round sanctuary, offers a clarity (clarté, like what the French Gothic masons were seeking—an interior contiguity or congruence with the exterior), which brings the whole of the early Renaissance (post Medieval) mind into easy acceptance of this cubic and spherical space. A wonder!

Frederick Hartt says the following of the ideals of Alberti brought to expression in Brunelleschi.:

> Rectangles and circles on a square plane are elements of architectural draftsmanship that are carried out with basic geometrical instruments, the compass and square: Brunelleschi's architecture has been called "paper architecture" and to some degree it does preserve in stone the procedures of laying out architectural shapes on paper. Indeed, this beautifully simple partitioning covers not only the principles but the message of Brunelleschi's architecture. After the complexity of the committee-built medieval structure, he leads us by degree into a new world of simplicity and order, clear-cut proportion and exact relationships. It is in the gigantic harmonies that Brunelleschi established for the Cathedral of Florence, rather than in the classical details which one makes out only at close range, that the individualism of the Early Renaissance is apparent. Especially the shape of the dome has an immense tension, resembling a Gothic vault more than the hemispherical dome of the Pantheon that Brunelleschi had studied and measured in Rome...the shape of Brunelleschi's dome suggests the new absolute of Early Renaissance, the idea of the indomitable individual will, whose autonomy the embattled Republic was trying to preserve, against seemingly unbeatible odds. (Frederick Hartt, History of Italian Renaissance Art: Painting, Sculpture, Architecture, Prentice-Hall and Harry N. Abrams, 1969, pg.114)

So, we have the impression that the architect has achieved something unique in the world, something which unleashes, a new way of looking at the world, a new way of designing church interiors. Brunelleschi's first big dome gives way to the simpler and more profoundly empty place with the flatter dome. The Pazzi Chapel is the Renaissance church par excellence.

The strange thing about the experience of this relatively early Renaissance edifice (1429-1446) is that it is so empty ! All of the artwork described by McCarthy is near the ceiling, somewhat like the Byzantine custom of leaving bare the marble walls at eye level and filling the heavens of the interior space with mosaics. The roundels here are, of course, few and delicately balanced, with little color to demand attention. They function almost as windows in the indirect and soft light from the windows of the magnificent simple-seeming, groin-vaulted dome.

In our own day there is a growing complaint that liturgical spaces are so often devoid of visual delight. Our modern white boxes, free from the pictures and statues which, done by a person who struggles at least as much to make sense of the gospel story in a visual realm as the preacher might in an auditory one, are quite barren. Brendan McCarhty in a recent issue of The Tablet, a British journal of Catholic opinion, quotes Fr. Oliver McTiernan, presently a Harvard research fellow and former pastor of an English parish with a heavy outreach to artists:

> There is minimal engagement by the Church with any of the arts, either visual or performing. We have simply stopped trying to find a spiritual message in the arts. We're almost frightened to try. The Jansenist legacy is still very strong Anything to do with physical or bodily expression is perceived subconsciously as an occasion of sin. (The Tablet 17 November 2001, pg. 1633)

The simplicity of the austerity faction, in conflict with the richness faction, found that a couple of prime examples of how a church, full of visual preaching or iconic presence, though successful, could be the exceptions which prove the rule.

The Upper Basilica of Saint Francis in Assisi has fresco cycles by both Cimabue and Giotto. The walls are full above a fresco of drapery. This again fits the Byzantine tradition of the plane lower walls, a human height wainscoting. Giotto has another such chapel in Padua, the Scrovegni Chapel. Fra Anagelico did one in the Vatican Palace itself. The Chapel of Nicholas V is a mini chapel full of beautiful paint well adapted to the meditations of a busy Renaissance pope. Julius II wanted to outdo that chapel and forced, as the story goes, Michelangelo to paint the fresco cycles of the Sistine Ceiling and the Last Judgment. Other such cycles were famously done by Tintoretto in Scuola San Rocco, Ghirlandaio in Santa Maria Novella, Caravaggio in the St. Matthew cycle in Saint Louis of the French in Rome, Piero della Francesca in San Francesco, Peter Paul Rubens in the Jesuit Church in Antwerp. All of these have plain wainscoting and great painted bibles above the heads of the congregants.

One way to look at artwork in churches is to consider them distracting because they are demanding. All of the works, mentioned as Renaissance gems above, would qualify as demanding attention. A great work of art is eloquent and rich, giving insight into meanings much deeper than the literal "read" of what they are about. Philosophers make distinctions between sacred subject matter and sacred art. All art which is really the expression of the human aspiration, the human psyche, is sacred because it is that. Art which purports to convince others of something but which has not got that spark, emanating from the spirit, is merely advertising, merely propaganda. Now the artwork of National Socialism has taught us that it is possible to do artwork that is propaganda and yet comes from the depth of human experience. But there is also "artwork" which comes from some place else There is "artwork" which can demand with only one purpose. "Artwork" which says "eat at Joe's," "smoke me," "buy me," is not artwork at all but tool. In Heidegger's distinction an artwork "preserves a world," whereas a "tool" merely performs a task, functions in a world (Martin Heidegger, "The Origin of a Work of Art," Poetry, Language, Thought, Trans. Albert Hofstadter, Harper & Row, 1971).

It is important to recognize that the Sistine Ceiling, for one instance, is usually backdrop for papal panoply. This would be quite significant theatre, ever since long before the Renaissance. Popes demand attention. The artwork, however, if one gets lost in it, continually leads to thoughts of God and the scriptural bedrock of Christianity. The arrangement of the dynamic thrust of all the works in the chamber would redirect the wandering eye back to the central ritual. The function of the artwork is to delight, to engage, to direct; it is not to distract but to focus.

Gail Wellborn, in a review of Paul Corby Finney, ed., Seeing Beyond the Word: Visual Arts and the Calvinist Tradition, Wm. B. Eerdmans, 1999 ("Christianity and the Arts," Vol. 8, No. 4, Fall 2001, pg.65) says, "John Calvin had an impact on all forms of art and architecture, bringing a stark, aesthetic look, yet Calvin himself did not express an avid interest in art except in what he termed 'external idolatry' and iconography. He feared it would detract from God and lead to idol worship." The Calvinist aesthetic, before there were any expulsions from the Church, was shared by many. This is shared sadly by many today.

In another book review in the same issue of "Christianity and the Arts" (pg. 63), Jeanette Hardage reviewing Steve Turner, Imagine: A Vision for Christians in the Arts, (Intervasrsity Press, 2001) describes Turner's visit "…to L'Abri, where his vision of what Christian art is became a liberating experience. That year was a turning point for him. It 'confirmed what I had instinctively felt for some time—that a lot of art created by Christians was bad and a lot of art created by non-Christians was good'." So, there is aftermath from the dominance of a particularly restrictive aesthetic—it seems to encourage entropy of art forms within a living organism, so that no art, or art of no substance, becomes the norm.

So many of the famous masterpieces of the Renaissance were done for churches and chapels in churches. Many of them are still in those churches. Many more are now in pieces, in a diaspora, to be found as lovely curiosities in the musea of the world.

In a recent issue of the New York Times Sunday Magazine (Deborah Solomon, The New York Times Magazine, December 9, 2001, pg. 73) the editors describe "The Year in Ideas: AN ENCYCLOPEDIA of innovations, conceptual leaps, harebrained schemes, cultural tremors & hindsight reckonings that made a difference in 2001." Solomon describes Calatrava's new pavilion at the Milwaukee Art Museum, with a reference to Gehry's Guggenheim Museum in Bilbao concluding, "…a museum with a nothing-special collection can become a sensation on the basis of its architecture."

The idea seems to have been borrowed by much of the modern Church as the leaders choose important architects to build wow-grabbing extravaganzas. The piteously surreptitious subtext in our modern world can be borrowed from the Times' description of museums and analogously attributed to too many of our churches: "As city planners everywhere have clearly realized, a museum can become a global attraction along the lines of the Tower of Pisa—and if the outside is good (and slanty) enough, it really doesn't matter what is inside."

Rudolph Arnheim says "In religious architecture, caprice has been offered almost unlimited liberty…" because of the competition in similar "barbarous imagery" and "ostentatious shape and color," the Church has sacrificed "the end to a highly dubious means" in order to "attract a dwindling clientele at almost any cost." (Dynamics, pg. 206)

Jeanette Mirsky also says of recent American church architecture:

> Houses of God built in the modern idiom are now found everywhere, and in a landscape filled with factories, supermarkets, amusement halls, and the like the surface resemblance of modern churches to secular structures seems to strip them of their sanctity, or make them seem in questionable taste or frankly profane..." (Houses of God, F.W. Dodge Corporation, 1957, pg. 144)

So the temper of the times seems to have changed quite a bit. It seems that many critics have found that the modern church, of the Church in the Modern World, leaves them cold. In our consideration of the progress into our own era, let us keep in mind that the older "renovations" were born in felt needs and came to express felt hopes about the world as it was, or as it might become.

Some Renaissance Developments

> No lay hand was allowed to touch it, even it that meant depriving a dying person of Viaticum. It was a very special favor when Popes of the fourteenth century gave to princes in certain instances the permission to touch the chalice on communion days with their bare hands. (Missarum Solemnia Vol I, pg. 128)

Thus, Jungmann gives us an impression of some of the results of the development of a sense of reverence for the Eucharist in the late Middle Ages. He also says:

> The holiest of the Church's possessions remained, it is true, the center of genuine piety. But also, the clouds and shadows surrounding this center brought matters to such a pass that the Institution of Jesus, that well of life from which the Church had drawn for fifteen hundred years, became an object of scorn and ridicule and was repudiated as horrible idolatry by entire peoples. (ibid. pg. 132)

He fleshes out the difficulties that led to the need for reform. The organ was "perfected" he says by the fourteenth century and began to be put into churches and cathedrals. The development of polyphony in Avignon was brought to Rome in 1377 when Gregory XI returned from the

"Babylonian Captivity." These both brought much dissent as some localities resented the introduction completely. Swiss monasteries, for instance, forbade polyphonic singing until as late as 1560. He says, "The designation of the fourteenth and fifteenth centuries as the 'autumn of the Middle Ages' (Huizinga) proved to be exceptionally apt in the history of the liturgy and not least in that of the Mass."(ibid., pp. 126 f)

Some Reactions to the Recent Past

Jungmann tells us that the Baroque period had some new developments that were a reaction to the experience of the Renaissance and the new self awareness which grew under the aegis of the great rebirth of classical principals.

> Private prayer was deliberately allied to public liturgy. (ibid. pg. 143)

Apparently fearing that an effort was being made to introduce the vernacular into the Mass, Alexander VII had in 1661 condemned a translation of the Roman Missal into French and had forbidden any further translation under pain of excommunication. (ibid. pg. 143)

> The mighty Baroque sermon was extended...Since the Middle Ages the site of the pulpit had gradually been altered, moved generally away from the altar and further into the nave. Like the sermon, it grew independent. (ibid. pg. 148)

> The place taken by the choir corresponds to this new situation—not in the choir from which it derives its name, but far away, on the boundary between the world and the church, in the organ loft. (ibid. pg. 149)

> Looking at the Host at the consecration no longer possessed the attraction and significance that it had towards the end of the Middle Ages. The new age sought not the sight of the holy, but the sight of the beautiful in art and universe. (ibid. pg. 150)

> The interior of the church has become a great hall filled with sensuous life. (ibid. pg. 150)

The next period, the Baroque, sees the growth of all these new "inventions" in the liturgical life of the Church. The Enlightenment follows close on the heels of the Baroque but interesting for our discussion is the reaction caused by that development. Interesting because we have been considering the swinging pendulum of the Renaissance and Baroque era. Remember Bazin's claim that all art history in the west can be seen as a swing from classical to baroque and back again? Well, Jungmann reminds us of the "Gothic Revival" in liturgy as a reaction to the Baroque/Enlightenment:

> In the dreary decades of the Enlightenment attempts were made, insensitively, to make worship conform with the ideas of rationality and utility. Thereafter it was not only Viollet-le-Duc who turned with a fresh enthusiasm towards the Middle Ages and ushered in a style of building, faithful to the models of that time. It was then that Prosper Gueranger declared war on all real or supposed distortions of the Roman Liturgy in France, and founded a center at Solesmes for the strict practice of this liturgy, especially of Gregorian chant. (Pastoral Liturgy, pg. 89 f)

Chapter Six: The Baroque Explosion

Reform brings conflicting expressions of the drive of the Church

The theological conflict in the church described at the end of the chapter on the Renaissance came to a head in the next era. The conflict of simplicity and richness found expression in the church of the post-reformation Baroque Era. On the one side were the decorated churches of the different Catholic Baroque cultures: on the other were those of the protesting ascetical reformers. Jungmann recounts:

> The holiest of the Church's possessions remained, it is true, the center of genuine piety. But alas, the clouds and shadows surrounding this center brought matters to such a pass that the Institution of Jesus, that well of life from which the Church had drawn for fifteen hundred years, became an object of scorn and ridicule and was repudiated as horrible idolatry by entire peoples. (<u>Missarum Solemnia Vol.I</u>, pg. 132)

Germain Bazin describes the reformers' churches as an "...intimidating nakedness...with their complete lack of images and ornamentation." (op. cit. pg. 98) Edwin Lynn characterizes all the ascetical Protestant churches when he describes those of the American Puritans in this way:

> Their religious architecture clearly showed their disapproval of other forms of worship. Puritans believed that an individual could directly contact a personal God. Life was orderly and without mystery, and God's radiance was everywhere. (op. cit., pg. 98)

For Catholics the winds of change were also making a difference. Jungmann:

> Looking at the Host at the consecration no longer possessed the attraction and significance that it had towards the end of the Middle Ages. The new age sought not the sight of the holy, but the sight of the beautiful in art and the universe. (<u>Missarum Solemnia Vol I</u>, pg. 150)

In fact in contrast, the superstitions of the Middle Ages made many a cluttered interior. The need for stipended masses had so multiplied that there were altars in every conceivable empty place in many churches. The year 1500 saw forty-eight altars, each, in the churches of St. Mary in Danzig and the Cathedral at Magdeburg. (Jungmann, Missarum Solemnia, Vol. I, pg. 224) Breslau in the fifteenth century had two churches with two hundred and thrity-six altars each! (Jungmann, Pastoral Liturgy, pg. 66) Indeed in his own jurisdiction, St. Charles Borromeo ordered the removal of altars from organ loft, pulpit, pillars, and all other such places. (Missarum Solemnia, Vol. I, pg. 224)

Other difficulties surfaced in the Renaissance which had to be dealt with. The role of music rose to unprecedented importance. Jungmann:

> What has been said holds true also for church music at this time. Here, too, the Mass was treated as self-contained. Music spread its gorgeous mouth over the whole Mass, so that the other details of the rite scarcely had and significance...
>
> It is significant that the princely courts, both great and small, were the first places where this type of church music was cultivated and where it reached its splendor. Because of the religio-cultural situation it sometimes happened that this church music, which had fallen more and more into the hands of laymen, forgot that it was meant to subserve the liturgical action.
>
> ...there were festive occasions which might best be described as "church concerts with liturgical accompaniment." (Missarum Solemnia Vol. I, pg. 148, f)

The later Baroque churches built for the Roman Rite had a sense of both order and accommodation, fruits of the Tridentine understanding of the value of the Mass in itself and of the reform to simplicity which was, after all, not only a reaction to illusory abuses in the Church but also a response to humanism-gone-wild in the later Renaissance.

The Jesuit Church of the Gesu

Germain Bazin says that there is always a contrast between the baroque spirit and the classical. Nietzche contrasts the mode of Dionysius with that of Apollo. Janson contrasts the romantic and the classical. Clark the terrestrial to the celestial feminine ideal.

The Church of the Gesu (1568-1584) is called by most art historians the "first church" of the Baroque period. Designed by Giacomo Della Porta and Giacomo da Vignola, it rises where the Church of Santa Maria della Strada had stood, a gift from the Pope to St. Ignatius. The Farnese pope, it seems, enamored of the new order, wanted its headquarters right near his own home, the Palazzo Venezia (which later became Mussolini's headquarters). Michelangelo, himself a devotee of St. Ignatius and a maker of the Spiritual Exercises, had proposed his own contributing of his services for the new church but the funding came only after his ability to do so had diminished.

Its exterior is of a double classical order with a pediment that is softened by great volutes gently opening, or closing, their nautilus to the sky. The façade opens onto a small piazza which gives it an urban space as forecourt. The pilgrim enters up the stairs into the temple from the very pavement of the city. S/he comes in under the organ loft, a place "...on the Boundary between the world and the church,..." (ibid. pg. 149)

The vaulted unbroken surface of the ceiling is today covered with a panoply of saints glorifying the Holy Name of Jesus, the painting by Gaulli with an ingenious frame of clouds bubbling out of the architectural frame itself. The saints and the heavens rise from this very nave into the apotheosis above. The painting is a tour de force rivaled often in Baroque interiors but never surpassed.

The church has side aisles and apsidal chapels at their eastern terminations but the piers separating the aisles from the nave are so thick that the nave is a completely independent space. The chapels along the side walls of the church are each in an independent compartment, appropriate for the many masses said at once in a sacerdotal community, and yet hardly impinging on the emotional space of the one church. There are two large altars in the pseudo-transepts. They commemorate the burial of St. Ignatius of Loyola on the left and the arm of his college roommate, St. Francis Xavier, on the right. The two memorials to the first Jesuit saints face each other and establish a dialogue across the nave directly in front of the sanctuary. In front is the "high altar" where the tabernacle resided under a painting or a sculpture of Jesus (alternating these days).

Presently there is a large moveable altar and lectern and presidential seat, having a presence but a temporary one in this magnificent museum church.

Jungmann tells us of the history of the pulpit. In the second century there were boys living in common, especially in Rome, whose job it was to be "lector." By the seventh and eighth centuries, reading had become the job of the sub deacon. By the thirteenth, the Epistle could be read by a Mass server. (All of the above is from Missarum Solemnia, Vol. I, pg. 410) Only bishops preached in the early years, an extension of their teaching authority; but the Council of Vaison, in 529 CE, made preaching a right of priests. In the Gallican liturgies preaching is normal. In 813, as part of the Carolingian Reform, synods demand a vernacular translation of the homily. (ibid. pg. 458)

There is a Baroque pulpit within the body of the nave. It seems to have become a common piece of church furniture since the time of the Franciscans and the Dominicans who made of preaching an apostolate and an occupation, respectable and, by the time of the Jesuits, Theatines, Oratorians, and Oblates of St. Francis de Sales, necessary as a major entertainment of the period. Of this piece of furniture Jungmann tells us that a "scaffold" became required for it in the Middle Ages. (ibid. pg. 460) He also tells us :

> In the church architecture of the later Middle Ages the ambo is no longer considered, or, to be more precise, it is moved away from the cancelli further into the nave of the church where it becomes a pulpit. (ibid, pg. 418)
>
> The mighty Baroque sermon was extended… since the Middle Ages the site of the pulpit had gradually been altered, moved generally away from the altar and further into the nave. Like the sermon, it grew independent. (ibid. pg. 148)

The Organ

The Renaissance is also the time of the development of new forms of music. It leads to polyphony and instrumental accompaniment. The organ is introduced with surprising results. Originally rejected as too secular, while the spiritually profound guitar was preferred, eventually the organ becomes the only instrumental voice of sufficient gravitas, spiritual weight or "gravity," to be permitted in the churches after the Missal of Pius V.

The Baroque and the Rococo which builds on the Baroque, develop as backdrops to theater, ballet, and organ music, as aids to preaching –along with the dominant stage of the Era, the Pulpit, which finds itself moving into the center of the audience chamber.

The great dome of the Gesu sits above the "crossing," where the transepts in elevation meet the nave and sanctuary. It sits so high and so close to the short arms of the cross that it seems to hover over the space of the whole church. A few short blocks away the similar Church of Saint Ignatius was a chapel to the Roman College, first site of that great Jesuit institution. Bernini re-architected the campo, the little square in front of the great façade so that the whole piazza could serve as theater for productions which would serve the Gospel as did the miracle and mystery plays of the Middle Ages. The walls of the surrounding buildings have an integration in bays and breaks which allow both a visual and an auditory unity, making a successful theater for ballet, opera, and drama. All of which exploded into the Jesuit approach to education, establishing a dramatic footing for the new era in European and colonial education for the masses. In fact, St. Ignatius' Ratio Studiorum, took the antique Trivium and Quadrivium and created a new approach which revolutionized the educational endeavor.

On the inside of this great Baroque chamber, Brother Andrea Pozzo created a total world with his ceiling painting, much like the building of the Gesu in both plan and elevation, this great church suffered from a lack of final funding. The dome, never built, left a virtual hole in the ceiling at the crossing. Pozzo virtually filled the whole with a tormpe l'oeil of a dome which, after its recent cleaning, is totally believable, at least from the proper point on the floor.

Problematically for the liturgy, this artistic tour de force takes over the attention of the pilgrim, making the domus a distraction. Yet the achievement stands as a metaphor for all the art of the Jesuit missionary effort. It makes the viewer realize that his or her view of the world might be inadequate because it does not account for the effect that this fake has on his or her psyche. Perhaps there is something to what these men are saying about the interior life in Christ! At any rate, the distracting tour de force is high enough above the sanctuary that, near the sanctuary, the pilgrim would not be aware of it.

Sant' Andrea al Quirinale

Gianlorenzo Bernini was an apprentice in the architectural "firm" of Donato Bramante, first master mason of the new basilica being built at St. Peter's. Bramante's nephew, Francesco Borromini, was also an apprentice. There developed an intense rivalry between these two genius designers. Bernini's take on the Baroque movement took his architecture into the realms of great size and decoration of surfaces. Boromini's went in the direction of manipulation of surfaces.

Sant' Andrea (1568-1570), the novitiate chapel of the Jesuits across the street from what is now the Presidential Palace of Italy and what was then the Papal Quirinal Palace. It is a little jewel, capacious for one hundred and fifty or two hundred congregants. Bernini, himself, considered this his masterpiece. The pilgrim enters up some rounded stairs through a rounded porch, then an inner vestibule, into a domed oval church. The coffered oval dome is crowned by a lantern surrounded by angels. Directly across the nave space is the sanctuary framed by a triumphal arch crowned with a broken segment, the place between the halves occupied by an ascendant St. Andrew. The sanctuary is behind four fluted, Corinthian columns; there is a smaller lantern pouring light onto the altar and walls and the golden rays of the sanctuary's marble frame for the retablo painting of the crucified Saint Andrew. The walls of the chapel are articulated by alternating rounded arches and square doorways, an homage to the Pantheon's grander alternations a few blocks away.

The marvel is clearly an influence on so many similar churches throughout the Baroque Italian world and it has its counterparts throughout what was then a colonial empire. The Jesuit churches in Bogota, Ciudad de Mexico, Asuncion in Paraguay all have a tangible Bernini influence. The continent, meaning Europe, also has thousands of such places. The continent, meaning North America, is full of Baroque Revival masterpieces. Built during the nineteenth and twentieth centuries, these great churches were a way to say that immigrant Catholics had a homeland of great cultural, economic, and political, as well as spiritual wealth! –the "homeland" being Bernini's Roman Catholic Church.

San Carlo alle Quattro Fontane

The other architect, Borromini built a chapel just up the Quirinal hill, at the corner of the street footed by the Barberini Palace. San Carlo (1638-1667) has a temple-like entrance to its regular floor plan on an irregular plot of land. The interior has plain-surfaced plaster walls. There are four altars, the one at the east end being higher and more ornate. The dome hovers over the entire space. The dome is coffered with larger forms at the base and smaller ones at the pinnacle, lending an impression of height to quite a small chapel. It offers the spirit a great deal of space but there is not much for the imagination to play with as there is in the Bernini chapel of similar size.

Borromini's Sant' Ivo and Santa Sapienzia are topped with dizzying lanterns, spiraling heavenward and lighted by glorious white light. The very epitome of imagination playing with rarefied space and no distractions is the Catholic expression of the Protestant effort toward Puritan reform. In a later century, following the French Revolution and the supremacy of The Enlightenment, and just after the "Reign of Terror," cathedrals in France lost the heads of the kings and saints, the bodies of nobles and royals from their tombs, and the very deity to whom the places were dedicated were dispossessed in favor of deified Reason. Some of those destroyed masterpieces still have a sense of unity and mystery because of the designers' following of Borromini's example.

Modern Examples of the two extremes?

Twisted spaces, churches without iconic focus but with marvelously playful space have become a progeny of Borromini's brilliance all over the modern world. Bernini, buried humbly at Sant Maria Maggiore, claimed there as "maker of the arts and of the world," becomes the architect of the past glories of the Catholic Church. The acclaimed stars of Rudolph Schwarz (Maria Konigen in Saarbrucken and St. Anna in Duren), Domenikus Boehm (St. Engelbert in Riehl), Gottfried Boehm (St. Albert in Saarbrucken), Alvar Aalto (Church in Riola di Vergato), le Corbusier (at Ronchamp), Oscar Niemeyer (Presidential Chapel in Brasilia), Michelucci (the Autostrada Church at Florence), Steven Holl (the Chapel of St. Ignatius in Seattle), and Richard Meier (The Church of the Year 2000 in Rome) have risen to make Borromini reborn as the great seminal genius of late Catholic Modernism expressed in the churches of a Post modern Enlightenment. Even Philip Johnson's Chapel of Thanksgiving in Dallas, with its spiraling tower and stained glass skylight, does in color what Borromini did in white and light. (Most of these buildings can be viewed in Edwin Heathcote and Ilona Spens, Church Builders.) There is, of course another tradition or two impinging on the present but Borromini's influence deserves its applause. Interestingly, most of these modern churches have a long liturgical plan, meaning the altar, ambo, and presidential seat are at one end facing the nave, rather than, in any way encouraging the encounter of community across the face of God as imagined at the altar between them.

Chapter Seven: Revival Churches

Fire's Fury and Building Booms

The Great Fire of 1666 in London, of course, released a flurry of architectural activity. Sir Christopher Wren is the name associated with the emergence of a whole new approach to church design. The catalogue designers Webb and Gibbs, building on the approaches of Robert Adam and Inigo Jones, were given a blast of energy by the implosion/explosion that the fire released in its aftermath.

There were other reasons for building in the seventeenth century, too. The Age of Exploration necessitated houses of worship for the use of the explorers. Other concerns made them opportune for the aims of imperialist colonialism which followed closely on the explorers' heals. Not all missionary work, of course, was motivated by colonialism or by what has come to be seen with twentieth century hindsight as cultural imperialism. There was a real motivation to help the "natives" know the Lord. The moral high ground was and can still be taken by those who wish to share the good news of Jesus Christ. It is, however, unique to the century of Dutch, English, French, German, Spanish, and Portuguese colonizaton that conquest became an endeavor fit for the testosterone of European men. The wars of religion added a certain creative gusto to the game. Mercantile companies also played a sectarian accompaniment, if you will, to the arias sung by the leading heroes of the century of exploration. So, there were many reasons for the building of churches. God suddenly had temples to counter the temples of the gods of the perceived infidels of the Americas but His temples also carried antagonistic political agenda.

Building on the sensible successes and delightful designs of Andrea Palladio, San Giorgio Maggiore and Il Redentore in Venice, the era of British colonial architecture, called Georgian, because it flourished under the reign of George III, produced Independence Hall in Philadelphia, the "Barracks" in Sidney, and multiple Christ Churches in the four quadrants of the British globe. The "palladian window" and the spare hall church with balcony and soft gray light became profligate all over the English speaking world. There were contrary colonial counterparts, "Spanish Baroque" being most noteworthy in South and Central America as well as the Philippines and the Asian sub-continents.

King's Chapel in Boston, Christ Church and Old St. Peter's in Philadelphia, Sts. Peter and Paul in Charleston are among the oldest English Baroque churches in the United States. There were Catholic counterparts in the next century. Old St. Joseph's in Philadelphia, St. Thomas Manor in Port Tobacco, Maryland, and Old St. Mary's in St. Louis were English Baroque buildings in essence. This implied that Catholics were now among the founding families. Even though their exteriors were more "Federal," these grand buildings began to put Catholics on the map in Protestant America. They are colonial buildings with a gloss of decades of Greek Revival.

English Baroque or Georgian construction followed upon the redevelopment of the homeland after the fire all in one fell-swoop. Its spread to the colonies was not especially pronounced since almost all the religiously endowed expeditionary forces produced buildings for worship in the Baroque mode. Most of the colonial traditions, Catholic or Protestant, are Baroque, since that was the given style. The avant garde of architectural taste was espoused in experiments proposed and funded by people too refined for the hard labor of conquest. The lands of European colonization have hall churches, good acoustics, pronounced pulpits, balconies. Some had paintings, sculptures, and stained glass. In the realms of the more sophisticated indigenous peoples, Inca, Aztec, Navaho, native artisans had profound effect on the decoration of the churches——these are mostly Catholic and mostly in Latin American urban centers.

The neo-classical-colonial-palladian-georgian-baroque style was the paramount building style of the Americas until the Revolution. Greek Revival had erupted in Europe. The British Museum of Robert Smirke and Karl Friedrich Shinkel's Altes Museum in Berlin as well as Soufflot's Ste. Genevieve all bespoke a new vocabulary with the old ideals of classicism. Napoleon's desires to show his heritage, successor to Egypt's pharaoh and Rome's emperor clearly established a new direction for the expression of different hegemonies in the Old World. Everyone wanted to be the successors to the great past, as they were seeing it again——a kind of northern Renaissance again.

Spiro Kostoff in A History of Architecture: Settings and Rituals (Oxford University Press, 1995) says of the American experience:

> ...Thomas Jefferson (1743-1826) was the great perceptor. Against the Federalist faith in a strong central government reliant on the new moneyed classes, Jefferson championed a democratic society of small landowners, an agrarian utopia. The capacity to give physical shape to this republican environment was locked within the people, he thought, and had only to be released through the proper incitement. The idealism, and the forms that could encapsulate it, should come straight from the roots, from ancient Greece and Rome—the source that had given revolutionary France her shoring symbols, and could do the same for the United States of America (pg. 618)

And so, a "Greek Revival," expressed in terms of Athenian Democracy and based on Roman Republican ideals, emerged at the time that the new federal city was being planned. Federalism also a housing style for the new Republic still had its churches being designed by great architects like Charles Bullfinch and Benjamin Latrobe. The nineteenth century, however, saw the introduction of Greek Revival facades with a baroque continuity on the interiors of churches. This occurred perhaps, because the churches of the American Catholic minority had only a mask of republican religion. Underneath, the religious traditions continued from the European bases, especially for the Catholic immigrants. Soon the interior continuity takes on an external manifestation in the Baroque Revival. Catholic immigrants came from "counter-reformation" centers, after all. Though their emigration was motivated by hunger for possibilities not available to them in their homelands, the new Americans looked back to their homelands for a sense of who they were. Thus Baroque Revival was not so much English, Georgian, Baroque but something larger—Italian, German, Spanish, Portuguese, Bohemian, Hungarian, Austrian, Polish, Russian, etc.

Revivals in the Immigrant Century

H.W. Janson speaks of twentieth century architecture in terms of its distinction from what went before:

> For more than a century, from the mid-eighteenth to the late nineteenth, architecture had been dominated by a succession of "revival styles"... This term, we will recall, does not imply that ear-

> lier forms were slavishly copied; the best work of the time has both individuality and high distinction. Yet the architectural wisdom of the past, however freely interpreted, proved in the long run to be inadequate for the needs of the present. The authority of historic modes had to be broken if the industrial era was to produce a truly contemporary style. (History of Art, Prentice-Hall, 1973, pg. 553)

Baroque Revival, Romanesque Revival, Gothic Revival, each had reverberant portents burgeoning from multiple cultural motivations. Romanticism and Neo Classicism were in dialogue in the midst of what had become part of a general trend by the height of the nineteenth century. A general reawakening to things of romance produced an intellectual approach to Liturgy. There was a reawakening of Gregorian Chant and other musical traditions. There was a new interest in whence liturgical traditions came and then in whither they were going. Eventually, the new intellectual movement in the Church aroused a discomfort with the felt stagnation of Trent and Vatican I.

James Renwick's St. Patrick's Cathedral is a Gothic Revival structure, built in the open in the 1850's, right in front of all the WASP founders. Thus, Archbishop Hughes would repel the brash response of the No Nothings, who in the 1840's had wrought havoc on the American Catholic landscape because of their fear of the papist threat. The old St. Patrick's Cathedral, downtown, had had a high wall built around it to repel the bullets of that crowd. This new edifice would say that the Catholics are here and here to stay. The New Cathedral of St. Louis (Barnett, Haynes, and Barnett) is a Baroque Revival masterpiece with an incredible Byzantine mosaic interior making that quasi-political statement in the very middle of the continent. Then, in the middle of the continent, the Catholic world has claim to a more distant past than it had claimed with the English baroque old cathedral. Benjamin Latrobe's Old St. Mary's is Baltimore is a Beaux Arts Baroque pantheon revisited on the American shore——surely linking the old seat of Archbishop Carroll, first Catholic bishop in the US, to the Roman imperial accoutrements of the Bishop of Rome. This must have threatened the most well-read of the No Nothings a great deal.

An American Church ?

Henry Hobson Richardson's Trinity Church is surely a Romanesque Revival building which brought the Brahmins of Boston thoroughly into the "modern era," reviving the romantic past of the Anglican Church. It was very different from the Congregational Churches of the post colonial establishment. So the romance and adventure of being American in the nineteenth century had effect in the churches built for many denominations.

Ralph Adams Cram's St. John the Divine, originally intended as the Episcopal byzantine cathedral, soon became the rival to St. Patrick's. It is even now, in its unfinished state, able to claim status as the largest Gothic cathedral in the world. John Frohman's Washington Cathedral is also Gothic. The really interesting thing about these two immensely beautiful cathedrals of the Anglican Communion is that they are not revival buildings at all, but constructed in masonry in the old ways, they can claim to be "authentic" in a way that the revival places (like St. Patrick's) cannot. These two have a claim on continuity with the mediaeval world in which the British Empire was born and whose culture still thrives in the old monied families on the new continent.

John Notmann in Philadelphia was a principal architect of three important revival churches. St. Clement's is a Romanesque Revival jewel with dark stained glass, great colorful but reserved statues, and heavy brown stone asymmetries throughout the parochial complex. Also asymmetrical, on the exterior, is his St. Mark's Episcopal, only a few blocks away and built only a few years later but as Gothic Revival masterpiece with Limoges stations of the cross and white marble statues (and a later spectacular Lady Chapel with silver antependium and retablo encrusted with silver figures in delicate Gothic poses). Then a few blocks away and a little later, Notman's collaboration with Napoleon le Brun stands as the largest church in the city, the Baroque Revival Cathedral/Basilica of Sts. Peter and Paul. This one is Italian with some mosaics and hardly any statues, very solidly built with no arcade level windows, perhaps as a protection from the still interested No Nothings. But this one architect seems to have embraced all the choices of the revival period and combined them to make both the Protestant and Catholic "new arrivals" in Quaker Philadelphia feel at home and somewhat in charge.

The Arts and Crafts movement playing with all the tools of the rivivals began to incorporate the tools of the Industrial Era. More and more architects began to deal with the austere authority of engineering. Emulating European culture because we now have wealth or because we came from a noble past. These are time-honored American motivations, claiming "arrival" for newly delivered immigrant populations. The communities which fled poverty or political unrest to seek a future in the "new world" brought their old experience of Church and tried different ways to preserve what they came from or to invent what they would now become.

The Mother Church of Christ Scientist in Boston, the Mother Bethel of the African Methodist Episcopal Church in Philadelphia, the Presbyterian masterpiece of Riverside Church in New York, Temple Bethel on Fifth Avenue, and Bryn Athen Cathedral of the Swedenborgians outside Philadelphia, these are all revival buildings with great "pedigrees." They attest to the wealth of their congregations but they also attest to an American commonality in their decoration. This means decoration, of course, aside from statues and paintings which had decidedly particular references.

Height of the Revivals

Revival buildings of all sorts had a momentum which led to a plethora of beautifully caparisoned pieces of architecture throughout the young rich republic. Saint Francis de Sales in Philadelphia is a Neo-byzantine jewel with a kind of beaux arts gloss making it both historic in appearance and "modern" in atmosphere for the twentieth century. Saint Vincent Ferrer in New York City achieves the same kind of urban grandeur but as a Gothic edifice. Saint Igantius Loyola in New York City has the mosaic "paintings" and terme windows of Roman and St. Petersburg Baroque. —— and the same elegant "feel."

There are a couple of capstone phenomena, buildings of international reputation which stand out as domus of the Americas. Saint Anne de Baupre, Our Lady of Guadalupe, The National Cathedral of Saints Peter and Paul (Episcopal) and the Cathedral Basilica of the Immaculate Conception (Roman Catholic) epitomize a national movement in the religious hegemonies of the American republics. They have a significance in our story because they give God a republican house to live in. So what do the revival churches give God that was not apparent when He occupied a throne in the imperial era, became a warrior in the Romanesque era, a relic in the Gothic, a godly Prince in the Renaissance, and an apotheosis of the manly God, persevering through the adversities of life and death in His humanity, in the Baroque?

The National Cathedral

The Washington Cathedral is a diocesan seat without a regular congregation occupying a large Neo-gothic place in the national capital. In the midst of a great garden forecourt full of large trees and shrubs, the cathedral is already in another world, sacred by comparison with its surrounding cityscape.

Entering under the undulating sculptures of Frederick Hart in the tympanum of the Westwerk, the pilgrim enters a spacious narthex with a glazed wall giving a glimpse of the vast interior space lighted softly by magnificent windows reflecting darkly off the white stone. The space of the nave has a false ending at the east end of the crossing with a rood screen cordoning off the great choir behind the immense pulpit. Actually the choir screen makes it impossible to see what is going on in the sanctuary unless one is in the middle of the nave, very near the center aisle. Progressive entry is evident but the clerical, canonical, choral communities have entry while the rest of the congregation must stay in the transepts and nave. This is evidence of the early start of this Gothic masterwork at the beginning of the twentieth century (1907).

There is often an altar placed at the crossing on the marble cross in the pavement. This one is then at the center of the axis and visible to all the congregation. This variation has been adapted at many large cruciform churches, noteworthy at Amiens, Notre Dame de Paris, Michaelskerk in Munich, the Cathedral of the Nativity of the Virgin in Milano. This has become an easy and natural arrangement at large cruciform churches where nave and crossing have not been cluttered with choirs and tombs and such. The choir, itself, is quite adequate for smaller liturgical events, including the prayer services of Matins, Lauds, Vespers and such devotions practiced by Episcopalians and others in the national cathedral.

A great metropolitan cathedral with the ability to be intimate at one moment and grand at another moment seems most appropriate. The decoration, windows, raredos, side chapels, all seem to work either as focus for one of the smaller spaces or as ambient but negligible furnishings when the focus is centralized in the great space. The place is a tour de force , as a cathedral built in the continuing contribution of the Gothic experience.

Robert Paul Jordan gives this account of his visit to the great cathedral:

> Washington Cathedral is, in fine, awesome. "Most families feel insecure, uncertain, at first sight," Mrs. Frank H. Hammond, head of visiting services, told me one morning. "it seems overwhelming. They wonder if they are free to walk wherever they like. Of course, they are. Soon they feel completely at home."
>
> I watched enchanted as chattering 3- and 4-year olds trooped in, a noisy gang, of happiness. Immediately they fell silent, grew wide eyed, looked about, looked up, began whispering. They had seen no place like this, with its vast hall, huge columns, and bejeweled windows. ("Washington Cathedral: 'House of Prayer for All People'," National Geographic, 157, no. 4, April 1980, pp. 552-573)

We have this impression that a city domus for the whole nation is alive and well on St. Alban's Hill, right there where the founding fathers intended the great non-denominational cathedral to sit.

The National Shrine

The Getleins bemoan the empty yearnings of a good deal of Catholic church builders in describing the Shrine of the Immaculate Conception. They say it is:

> ... a nostalgic harkening back to former Catholic glories, with the underlying, despondent assumption that the days of Catholic artistic glory are gone forever; the best we can do today is make endless and endlessly ingenious copies of what the Church could bring into being when it was alive. (Frank and Dorothy Getlein, Christianity in Modern Art, The Bruce Publishing Company, 1961, pg.113)

There is, somehow, a different sense to this place. There is a sense of having been betrayed in this commentary of the Getleins. In 1964 Pope Paul VI virtually acknowledged the truth of their attitude when, in an address to artists on the feast of the Ascension, he said for himself and his predecessors of this century: "We have insisted on this or that tradition to be followed; we have set up these canons from which you must not deviate; we have oppressed you at times as it were with a cloak of lead...For this we beg your pardon." (C.J. McNaspy, S.J., Our Changing Liturgy, New York: Hawthorne Books, 1966, 128).

So we have an impression that there is something false about the artwork in the National Shrine whereas there is something authentic about the artwork of the National Cathedral. And yet, the size is comparable, the respect for the past is comparable, and the age is comparable. What is different is that the decoration is too much of a distraction in the one and fits so well in the other.

The appropriateness of decoration in the domus seems to rest on some almost ineffable happenstance of grace. Perhaps the only difference is taste. Youthful observers often notice that "Episcopalians have it and Catholics don't." Perhaps it is more complex. This discussion is not within the realm of our present task but it should be well worth a few years of dialogue in schools of theology and academies of architecture!

Is not the American domus for God, exemplified in these revivals. a throwback to old ideas of divinity? Is it not somewhat evident that a new approach should be happening?

God Gets What from the American Church?

The one thing that seems to dominate the revivals in the United States is that a lot is spent to build God beautiful houses all over the new rich Republic, giving God in each place prestige in the world community. Each immigrant group claims God as their own. Transcending denominations, God becomes an American!

Old World Developments and a New World Coming into Its Own

In marked contrast to the developing need for brakes on political, commercial, social, movements being given impetus by the inventions of the modern era. A fear was unleashed opposing the exuberant reception at the opening of Joseph Paxton's 1851 Crystal Palace, of the products of "industrial arts." Many in the western world agreed. Popes Pius IX and X recommended the importance of looking backward to the roots of the Church for inspiration in the arts as well as in polity. Prince Albert's great exhibition in Great Britain, celebrating Victoria's years of Empire, exhibited industrial products from all over the Empire; the message: machines could make a better world. The machine-made wonders were, however, not yet comparable to the products of human hands and there was a counter-movement. The movement in architecture produces a gateway for the twentieth century in church design.

Not until the Arts and Crafts Movement in England, a kind of cultural rebellion against the crass nature of "machine made arts," had arrived in the US, did the Americas begin to produce a culture that combined folk traditions, building in the hearts of the landed citizenry, with the austerity of high culture. Art Nouveau and Beaux Arts Neo Classicism in Europe had imitators in the US but after the industrial revolution, they blossomed into full flower. A new self-awareness following World War I, gave birth to a new beginning. "I coulda been a contendah" from Marlon Brando's mouth in <u>On the Waterfront</u> captures the thought; what birthright had not given the US, wealth and strength now bestowed. America began to find its cultural voice.

This movement takes the advances in Europe made by August Perret, le Corbusier, Rudolph Schwarz, Gottfried Boehm, Otto Wagner, Walter Gropius, Ludwig Mies van der Rohe, Alvar Alto, a movement epitomized in Mies' phrase; "Less is more," and brings about a new simplicity in church design. The work of Daniel Burnham, Lewis Sullivan, Frank Lloyd Wright, leading in a similar direction, was motivated by the allure of an industrial future full of economic promise. Their movement also has an immortal catchphrase, Sullivan's "Form follows function."

The Roaring 'Twenties produced an independent American intellectual and cultural movement. Art Deco was part of a first wave of creativity, followed by "modernism" and "post modernism." American culture began to produce its own churches. The American century began to produce its own church tradition.

Chapter Eight: Today's Church

The Difference Between Revivals Before the Bomb and After

Consider these gems: Auguste Perret's Notre Dame du Raincy, le Corbusier's Notre Dame du Haut at Ronchamp, Domenikus Bohm's Church at Nordeney, Rudolph Schwarz' St. Michael in Frankfurt, and his Maria Konigen in Saarbrucken, Karl Moser's St. Anthony in Basle, Marcel Breuer's St. Louis Priory in St. Louis Missouri, Otto Wagner's Saint Leopold in Vienna , Pietro Belluschi's St. Mary's Cathedral San Francisco, Oscar Neimeyer's Cathedral of Brasilia, Aarnu Ruusuvoric's Church in Hyrinkaa, and Alvar Aalto's Church in Riola di Vargato. These are the seminal gems of modern church architecture, all lovely spaces, but without iconic presences. This modern history has informed the "modern" and "post-modern" period with a quasi-mandate to propagate more iconoclastic, idealistic, barren barns for God. Is this a kind of "post Christian" response to the post modern world.

St. Andrew's and St. Kevin's Churches

Flushing, New York is the suburban community where I grew up. Queens is one of the boroughs of the City of New York and one of the counties of the State. When my parents were young this was farmland. Presently it is sprawling suburb becoming urban. There is precious little open space, lots of single family dwellings, many rows of attached housing, apartment houses, and shopping complexes, strip malls, restaurants, and fast-food places and street-side shops. When Denise Scott Brown and Robert Venturi wrote about Speedway in Tucson, Arizona as the epitome of drive-by American culture and spoke of similar speeding vehicular experience in Learning from Las Vegas (Robert Venturi, Denise Scott Brown, and Steven Izenour, M. I. T. Press, 1972), they might well have been talking about Northern Boulevard in Flushing, New York.

There are two churches there which indicate for me a change in the way that New Yorkers built their churches between the wars and after. The Church of Saint Andrew, built in 1926, sits in a suburb not far from where the film studios of New York were thriving and in the neighborhoods where the early stars built their homes. Big names like Valentino, Charlotte Greenwood, and the Dolly Sisters adorned houses all around this area when the Catholic community built this church. Thomas Merton was living just beyond the neighborhood in Port Washington and commuting through it on his way to the big city. F. Scott Fitzgerald described riding through this neighborhood in The Great Gatsby in rather run down terms. It was not where the wealthiest lived but where those with aspirations might find a great home —and build a great church.

Saint Andrew Avelino

St. Andrew's is a brick and marble complex with Spanish tile roofs on church, rectory, convent, and school. There is wrought iron fence, surrounding the entire parochial complex, with brick, limestone-capped stanchions. There is an Art Deco feel to the immense rondel of gilt bronze over the portal; it is mounted on a black marble, arched façade. The entrance up some steps and into a dark vestibule opens into a darkly mysterious space with alternating ruby, emerald, and ultramarine windows in the clerestory. The long plan and elevation has a northern orientation. The sanctuary has a baldachin over the tabernacle. A large pulpit with shell-shaped sounding board overhead was most evident and thrilling during my minority. There is, now, also a large marble baptistery with immersion font in the middle of the nave to one side. There are marble statues of the Virgin and the Sacred Heart. The whole interior is fitted with bronze accoutrements in the chandeliers, fences, window treatments in the ambulatory.

Designed in 1937 by Henry McGill, it a monument to the Art Deco inspiration from so many Hollywood facades and interiors. It speaks of an industrialized way of looking at design coupled with the romance of a growing place in the world. The automobile, the ocean liner, the zeppelin, the airplane, and the locomotive were the things which inspired the architects of movie sets and theaters to build such Spanish colonial mini-mansions as appear in the church's neighborhood.

There is a clarity to the elegance which speaks of Art Deco influences; in fact, Shreve, Lamb, and Harmon's Empire State and William van Alen's Chrysler buildings were being built in just the previous few years, a few miles west in Manhattan. The feel of the towers is of something modern, industrial, forward-looking, not exactly theatrical like all those theatres being built for the devotees of the film experience, whose initial home was, remember, right here on Long Island. The Spanish colonial church feels immediately appropriate to its time.

So the building is of its time. All the atmospheric and archetypal elements are present in a kind of basilican hall. This church has focus and elegance which made a lot of sense for the congregation who had "made it" during the hegemony of the Tridentine Mass.

Saint Kevin of Glendalough

St. Kevin's also had built a church. A few miles east of St. Andrew's, its 1926 building was a clapboard hall with amber glass in eight-light double hung sash windows. There was a vestibule of sorts behind the green doors. The sanctuary was at the southern end of the hall with a proscenium arch painted with life sized saints, the four evangelists. There were large side altars of a white painted wood. The main altar was similar with receding stepped shelves for twelve large candlesticks beside the tabernacle. The white, wooden mensa faced the wall. The priest never sat and so there was no seat. There were larger-than-life white marble statues of the Crowned Virgin and Child at one side and Saint Joseph at the other. There were also life-sized statues of the Sacred Heart, Saints Theresa of Lisieux, Anthony, and Kevin. There was a rather large crucifix with glass eyes and little teeth at the communion rail, a rood of sorts, but to the side.

This Saint Kevin's was obviously a farm house church and it stood for a quarter century as the parish church just a few miles from the magnificent Saint Andrew's. The parish complex grew to include a brick school with limestone caps and later a similar convent. Then the "good fathers" allowed the need for a new church to result in a brick and limestone rectory with slate roof and a large church built in 1957, by William J. Boegel from Rambusch, just before the Vatican Council.

This Saint Kevin's is entered right from the public sidewalk. Up a few steps one enters the bronze doors to see a flight of steps up between large piers, then a landing leads to a separate baptistery to the west while the leaded glass wall under the organ/choir loft allows a full view of the interior. A vast white space with peaked roof in furniture-finished paneling is inviting; it is full of light. The clerestory windows have figure stories in stained glass with gray areas outside all the figures. There is coining around the windows and the glass mimics the masonry in imagery and color. The south wall has a large wooden baldachin over the steps where the original face-the-wall, marble altar stood. It has been moved into the space closer to the false crossing (formed by transept walls higher in elevation than the windows in the ambulatory though in plan the place is a large hall). The marble altar with mosaic emblems on its frontispiece rests between the large, transept rondels with poly-foiled tracery frames making a suggestion of rose windows. There is a wooden pulpit. There are niches with simple mosaic walls at the sides of the proscenium wall for diminutive, three-foot-high statues, one of the Virgin with hands clasped, the other of Saint Joseph with right angle and plane. They stand on corbels like those of the main rood/raredos. Three-foot-high statues of Mary, John, and the Crucified sit in a wooden framed box on a field of tapestry, looking like a popular rose colored brocade table cloth. The statues are of a store-bought variety; their like can be found in Blessed Sacrament, Saint Mary's, Sacred Heart, neighboring churches built in much the same style.

This St. Kevin's has a similar sized church in the basement. Each "church" holds a thousand congregants in its nave. The difference in the lower church is that it has fluorescent banks of light on the vast ceiling which is only twelve feet over the heads of the entire congregation. The sanctuary is furnished similarly to the upstairs church but smaller with traceried wood paneling in a pseudo Tudor style. The altar and ambo are also wood. The crucifix is also much smaller. The walls of the nave are glazed orange yellow brick, the size of concrete blocks. There are windows (full of air-conditioners) at the tops of alcoves along the sides of the nave. The alcoves have the old marble statues from the old church; a couple of them have been painted very colorfully.

This church, with its two chambers, is really no competition for the complex at St. Andrew's, except that it holds many more people.Its Gothic references are much simplified, downplayed, made to seem more "modern." The statues in the upper church seem no longer monumental but decorative. They do focus the congregation but they do not command respect as did the old statues from the older church, now consigned to the basement. The windows are much more detailed than the reds and blues of St. Andrew's but they can take the eye of the congregants who are, after all, very distant from the sanctuary with its little statues. Since the windows do not point in any way toward the sanctuary, the become a distraction because they are so much more commanding than the rood. Whereas St. Andrew's has extensive stencil work and painted panels along with marble and tile flooring, St. Kevin's has very plain walls and terrazzo except in the sanctuary.

So there is a sense that this place is less focused than St. Andrew's even though there are all those things that would make it appropriate for liturgy. There is ascent to the holy-of-holies in a monumentally cavernous place. Profusion is evident in the windows, pews, corbels for the wooden roof. It is empty, silent, but not very dark. The stone, water, sky, tree are all depicted in the windows but the wood of the ceiling and the paneling of the sanctuary add a forested warmth to the otherwise cold interior. The problem with this vast space for liturgy is its emptiness. Because of the relative insignificance of the statues, and the great height of the nave and sanctuary, the cosmic center is not commanding. One can pay attention to the altar but one can easily be distracted by the congregation or the windows. So the place doesn't quite work.

The lower church is an altogether unworthy place for comment in this book. Except that it is a real pointer to how this building fits its congregation in a way that says much about the just-before-Vatican-Two American Catholic world. The revival had become vapid. The strip mall and its plain, beyond utilitarian simplicity had become the norm for "culture" in our land. The focus on God had become downplayed so much as to become unnoticeable. At the same time this place cost a great deal; the quality of the accoutrements was the best that middle-class suburban civility could find. This basement would be cooler in summer, warmer in winter, and can be used in much the same way as a "play room," "rec room," or "family room" would be used in the "finished basement" of a suburban home. Las Vegas of the 'fifties would be the vacation spot of choice for people who would feel perfectly at home in this "profane" basement church.

Venturi and Scott Brown might think this place most appropriate for American church goers! It seems an aberrant conclusion from John Dewey's "pragmatism" which makes no room for what has no practical use. The principle exchanges taste for utilitarianism!

Utilitarianism Gone Wild

On Manhattan's lower east side, the firm of Genovese and Maddalene built the Church of the Nativity to replace a decrepit Greek Revival church orignially built on the site in 1849. The older building had fallen on rough times. Long after its construction in a prosperous part of the port city of New York, it had become a parish in the down and out section of the city. Its balcony had been removed in order to prevent a collapse. Its devotional life, however, had proliferated within its walls. Countless statues lined its inner sanctum, a large hall with an old fashioned coram muro, facing-the-wall, altar on its east end. In the move to modernize the clergy and the leadership of the parish had agreed to remove some of the statues. After some hew and cry that plan was postponed. When the building was condemned and the new church planned, the old statues were put out on the trash heap on the sidewalk in front of the rectory. The modernization was going to proceed with a fury.

This is, for me, a watershed story, telling of the harsh political reality within the Church around the time of Vatican II, telling of the need for a council. People had become insensitive to the needs and wants of the opposition. Camps of Church people had decided that the opposition was "unsophisticated," enough so that there could be no dialogue about the future, only power plays would work. When this attitude pervades, the Church really suffers. The meaning of the term "Church Militant" refers to the primeval battle between Michael and Satan——not really to the battle between believers about the place of devotion in the building.

This is, however, a perduring political reality within the Church. It arises at transitional times when the whole world seems to have come to a point of new understanding about reality. In the Church those times arose with the Iconoclast Heresy during the eighth century, with the Great Schism of the tenth and eleventh centuries dividing the Church into east and west, with the twelfth century developments of monasticism and Gothic architecture, in the sixteenth century with the reform movements of Calvin, Zwingli, Luther, in the eighteenth century after the Reign of Terror, and in the nineteenth century with the revival of nationalism and the post Vatican

I romantic restoration of the roots of liturgy. It lives today after the Vatican II aggiornamento. There are those who want devotional images and those who do not.

There may, indeed, be a reluctance to deal with the contamination of images in the world, today. It seems that with the number of white boxes there is reason to think that. Is it because of the rise of the scientific mindset which will accept as fact only what it can prove? Is the "problem of faith" to be solved by a psychological or biological inquiry? Is it because with the rise in status of the Catholic intellectual, we have become embarrassed by the peasant quality of devotional practice? The disappearance of vigil candles and other votives from most urban churches cannot, however, counter the perennial wisdom that the encounter with the Mystery is profoundly simple, primitive even, the "mystery of faith."

New controversies about the origin of the world have overshadowed the old controversies about the nature of God. Only those who are not sophisticated enough to see the absurdity would engage in rosaries, or stations of the cross. Those unsophisticates watch televangelists with as much enthusiasm as they watch other talk show phenomena. We, who are above being bamboozled by anything anybody would say about the matters of the heart, are serenely secure in our clean and well-designed interiors wherein we attend to the very possibility of the deity with adequate reserve, while we afford ourselves therein a comfortable communal experience of the rites of passage, like weddings, funerals, baptisms. But we don't engage in any of that hokey-pokey falderol.

Immaculate Conception Ukranian Cathedral

The Ukranian Cathedral of the Immaculate Conception is a large dome on the cityscape of North Philadelphia. It is gold in color and low but vast in appearance on the skyline as one approaches from the raised Interstate 95. The reinforced concrete structure has a clean look as one ascends the steps and enters one of the three portal doors. There is a spacious narthex full of light. Through the glazed wall one enters a large space with an immense dome hovering overhead. The stained glass windows are not pictures; they color the daylight and make us aware that the sky is just outside. The whole place seems airy and light. The iconostasis has brilliant colored icons and the sides and ceiling of the dome have brightly colored and well drawn mosaics. The floor shines whitely while the gold glistens. The altar is directly behind the royal doors under the deesis but there are holes in the iconostasis so that there is a sense that the eucharist is happening among the people just as it would be in a western church. This cathedral is for a Ukranian rite denomination but, affiliated with Rome, it has the adaptations of the Vatican Council incorporated into its design. Even though the altar is at the western end instead of under the middle of the dome, the whole space seems to be covered by the single vault because of the height and because of the penetration of the iconostasis.

There are ways that a long plan can feel like a circular one. This cathedral is one of the best examples. Like the cathedral of St. Isaac in St. Petersburg, the whole is under the one dome. Even though the iconostasis in St. Petersburg is much more impenetrable and the light is very dim, there is a sense that the whole is one. It is especially so in the cathedral as museum because the royal doors are always open revealing the massive stained glass resurrected Christ.

The dome in Philadelphia is, however, low and flat more like the Hagia Sophia in Istanbul than like the Renaissance high domes of St. Peter, St. Paul, St. Isaac, and Our Lady of the Flowers. It follows the skyline profile of Frank Lloyd Wright's Annunciation Greek Orthodox Church (1959) in Wauwatosa, Wisconsin. This church can be viewed in Kennedy's American Churches (pg. 272f) That church looks to most like a spaceship and seems to clarion the superiority of Russian culture, which had recently put the sputnik in space under the Soviet auspices.

New Directions After the Vatican Council

The Second Vatican Council opened the doors and windows of the Church to let in the Holy Spirit. Aggiornamento, John XXIII's calls to reawakening, called the ancient Church toward a "today experience."

Ludwig Mies van der Rohe was one of those exiled genius architects from Germany. He had designed the Barcelona Pavilion for the Weimar Repbulic in 1929. Steel, marble, concrete and glass along with a pool and a singular statue, seemed to float in its surrounding pool and with its cantilevered entrance steps. It has an iconic function for architectural history. It is the quintessential glass box. Mies built a glass box chapel at the

Illinois Institute o f Technology in Chicago in 1952. Spare, empty, and gloriously focused, it proclaimed new possibilities for American architects.

It was soon followed by Eero Saarinen's Kresge Chapel at MIT in Cambridge (1955). This architect had been working in the United States with his father Eliel Saarinen for decades and had been influenced by both the Bauhaus aesthetic and the American penchant for simple pragmatism in structure. The form-follows- function aesthetic of Louis Sullivan which had been transformed by Lloyd Wright's "usonian" and prairie style houses into an American expression of the less-is-more aesthetic of Mies. The MIT chapel is a round brick structure with eyelets of windows at its base, giving it lift. This image of lift carries over later into Saarinen's landmark TWA terminal at what had been Idlewilde and is now JFK International. The interior of this non-denominational chapel has a shimmering light - filled sculpture by Harry Bertoia hanging like rectangular crystals of ice or smoke articulating the holy-of-holies as the space above the altar Against the undulating brick wall it seems to bring all attention to itself and the altar in front of it. The plain marble-block altar is up three steps on a marble plinth. There two pulpits, one on either side. The light filters through an oculus in the center of the ceiling (like the Pantheon). The undulating brick wall makes a very strong statement and welcomes the visitors.

Both of these buildings are beautiful and have a tremendous sense of holiness according all the atmospheric and archetypal requirements of liturgical space their due. They impinge significantly on the architectural programs of later American Catholic churches.

The commissioning of Mark Rothko by the de Menil Family foundation for a Catholic Chapel at Rice in Houston in 1964 resulted in a spare building designed by Philip Johnson, Howard Barnstone, and Eugene Aubrey. Entered through a basically unlighted, plain walled vestibule, the large white space with light filtered down from above onto the fourteen stations in marvelously violet and cobalt blacks is focused on four benches. There might have been an altar and ambo in this place, if the plan had survived the politics but the marvelously spare holy space is dedicated to peace rather than to God.

The de Menils had been in dialogue with Fr. Marie-Alain Couturier, OP who had been the principal motivator behind the French interlude of entertaining great artists to build God houses of worship, even if they were not Catholic. Couturier's monumental efforts resulted in the chapels at Assy, Ronchamp, Vence. Artists, Georges Braque, Henri Matisse, Fernand Leger, Marc Chagall Georges Rouault, and le Corbusier all worked on these three Catholic churches because of his untiring vision and conviction. Judith Dupre (Churches, pp. 120f) tells this story and ends it with a curious realization:

> In recent years, hugely publicized controversies like those surrounding works such as Andres Serrano's Piss Christ (1987) or Chris Ofili's Holy Virgin Mary (1996), which incorporated urine and elephant dung, respectively, ignited seemingly overnight. The merits of those particular works aside, the furor they generated, increasingly typical, have made it risky for church administrators to commission artists who might create incendiary works. It is far easier to go with those who will translate religious iconography in a less transcendent but comfortably inoffensive manner. In a society increasingly awed by technology and divorced from intuition, it does not seem possible for the rebirth of sacred art on the large scale once envisioned by Couturier to occur. (pg. 121)

Other Small Chapels

Tadao Ando has built small straightforward cubic spaces. The Chapel on Mount Rokka in Kobe, the Church on the Water in Hokkaido, and the Church of the Light in Osaka. These are chapels not for Catholic worship but they are so significant because of the way that Ando arranges the progressive entry through mountainscape, countryside, and cityscape, respectively, to bring the pilgrim to a place of significant focus, to listen, to meditate, to pray. Each has a cross as the most important visual structure but they are extremely austere—Zen almost. On descending through the chambers from the entrance to the chapel itself, the visitor centers him or herself. Entering the chapel, one descends toward the wall on which hangs a spare cross form. That is where the altar is and two chairs. The light is filtered and though one realizes the loveliness of the place s/he has passed through to get to the chapel, s/he experiences being within, somehow the land and lighted from above.

In his other small chapels the cross is more evident. On the water, the cross seems to walk on water. Across an empty wall and on the water, the cross is outside while the congregation is under the roof, in an enclosed and relatively dark place. The cross is in a beautiful natural setting and free. The Church of the Light has a cruciform opening in the concrete wall behind the desk/altar. The simple four squares of solid wall seem miraculous in that they stay apart in silent abeyance while the cross lets light into the sanctuary.

These are powerful spaces, strongly suggesting the power of the infinite who is ineffable except for the cross of the One who died on it. Meditative, contemplative, these places would refresh the visitor who came merely to bask in silence. They might also serve for liturgies of the Eucharist and the Word without distracting, but most they serve a purpose beyond that of ritual making congregations.

The Fay Jones experience is quite different. The glass walls and ceiling of Thorncrown or the Mildred Cooper Memorial Chapel make a statement of profusion of panes of glass and structural wood but the environment of woods and sky is what makes his places so wonderful. The presence of nature so engages the congregants that they are aware of some primeval presence with hardly any need to concentrate. The warmth and dry of being inside is a grand experience. Much like but nowhere near as intellectually arrived at as the Tadao Endo environments, Jones establishes a union with nature while inviting focus by the very design of his long halls within the environmental cathedrals of nature.

The Long vs. the Round Plan

The only thing that disturbs us in visiting these small chapels, large churches, and massive cathedrals is that they are almost all designed with a long plan. There is the place where the sacred is considered and there is the place where we sit. The Vatican Council II did recommend that the people now attend liturgy within a context of other people. The movement to a circular plan with the sanctuary in the middle is, as Roger Kennedy points out in a chapter called "Mandalas" (American Churches pg. 135 ff), is rather an old one. He quotes da Vinci and indicates the agreement of Bramante and Michelangelo when the papal basilica was being designed for a new St. Peter's. He also cites Saarinen's St. Louis Priory as a prime example of how this approach should work.

So many new Catholic places built after the Vatican Council II are still designed with a long plan. Alavaro Siza's Santa Maria in Marco de Canavezes, Portugal, receives a lot of praise. It is quite beautiful as one can see (Dupre, pp. 131 f or Heathcote and Spens, pp. 202-207). It has a very plain interior with spectacular architected clarity in square clerestory windows but a straightforward plan. Steven Holl's Chapel of St. Ignatius at Seattle University (Dupre, pp. 152 f or Heathcote and Spens, pp. 186-193) is also becoming quite famous. It, too, has a long plan with the sanctuary at one end. There is a crucifix on the wall to focus the congregation but there is no other decoration but color (like the Managua Metropolitan Cathedral of Legorreta).

Cesar Pelli's plan for St. Thomas More Chapel at St. John's University in Queens, New York (Dupre, pp. 156 f) will have an almost central sanctuary with seating almost in the round within a high spare octogonal space, widening at the ambulatory level. It, too, will have no images but a skylight which will travel down the (east?) wall making a Tadao Ando-like statement about the intrusion or incarnation of heaven or sky outside.

The church in the round with the congregation seeing its ritual center as the Table of the Lord against a backdrop of the Body of Christ is an almost untried but beautiful image of where the Church should have gone after Vatican II. One wonders why that has happened in so few liturgical spaces.

Saint Mary's Cathedral SF

Pietro Belluschi's Cathedral of St. Mary in San Francisco is a tremendous attempt of the twentieth century Church in America to build a major non-derivative piece of architecture in an urban setting. The pilgrim enters the church from an imposing plaza at the top of a hill overlooking downtown San Francisco. It is a wide, open and airy space whose eastern end is commanded by a quadripartite, tent-like, parabolic structure of pre-stressed and reinforced concrete. It soars heavenward from the plaza continuing the attitude of the hilltop.

One enters to discover under the sculpture of the doors a wide, dark inner narthex at whose center is a baptismal pool with living water. The font is in the center of a dry, marble pool into which descent is restrained by chains across the steps. Two rosewood in-houses, aedicules, form the gathering space between them but they do not reach the ceiling.

The parabolic four parts of the coffered ceiling seem to meet in a glass trough full of light, forming a cross at the pinnacle. The vast cavernous space is penetrated at the end opposite the font by a shimmering sculptural baldachin of light. This mimics the MIT baldachin but is much grander, higher, more electric in its presence.

The sanctuary is articulated by another rosewood in-building behind it. In front of that plain rosewood retablo are the principal pieces of furniture, a very large plain marble table altar has a reverberation of its design in the pulpit to the left and in the presidential thrones to the right.. There is another set of thrones above and behind the altar.

To the left of the sanctuary is a castle-like shrine for the blessed Sacrament. To the right is a mosaic and wood triptych representing the Virgin of Guadalupe, patroness of the Americas. To the outside corners ones eye wanders and there beholds a cityscape below the hill on which the cathedral sits. The cloud formations are beautiful but the windows do call to the eyes, unless there is something within to hold their attention.

Further to the right of the sanctuary, taking up the whole of the space on the right side of the chamber is a massive sculptural presence. Two stories of organ pipes and the raised console demand to be watched, even with any music emanating from it. Its presence rivals all other presences in the building.

Paul Heyer describes the achievement:

> As art and religion, each in its own way, seek to interpret the meaning or essence of our existence, so must religious architecture seek the essence of space, thinks Belluschi. "That is why space in a church acquires supreme importance," which Paul Tillich refers to as "holy Emptiness." …He searched for a form that would be high enough in the interior to provide the quality of space…He needed a form that would have height, dimension and drama, without bulk….A church "should strive to express its purpose, "

says Belluschi; in a building type where practical considerations may be important but are certainly not paramount, this presumably implies being both simple and profound, at peace and yet moving. And while a church must be intimate, "it should be a segment of space which reminds the worshipper of the infinity from which it was wrested, " says Belluschi. "integrity, proportion and clarity—it is through them that Beauty will shine." (Architects on Architecture: New Directions in America, Allen Lane, Penguin Press, 1967, pp. 232f)

There is a problem not envisioned by Belluschi thinking that "practical considerations may be important but are certainly not paramount." The practical considerations of the placing of the iconic presences and archetypal furniture, left to others, more precisely to the clergy. Actually, left to the whim of any presbyteral use or any sacristan on the payroll, practical considerations become, if not paramount, at least capable of destroying Tillich's "holy emptiness" as well as Belluschi's, and in the final analysis, lack of consideration results in no one's being able to pray without significant attention to ignoring what is going on around him or her.

The Metropolitan Cathedral of Managua

Ricardo Legorreta, on the other hand, commissioned by Thomas Monahan, the Domino's Pizza magnate, designed a new cathedral for the earhtquake and politically ravaged capital of Nicaragua. This building leaves nothing to chance, everything was prescribed. The bomb-resistent cube with multiple little domes is also a new direction for "holy emptiness" in the Americas.

This is a coffered reinforced concrete structure with most of the light coming from the lights in the sixty-three domes. There is strong color on some of the walls, an apse at the end of the space opposite the entry. There is no color on its rounded back wall. An ancient crucifix resides in a bullet domed chapel, separate from the main cube of the cathedral. It is penetrated by seemingly countless miniscule windows. The crystal dome over the crucifix picking up light from every source and making a shimmering presence, a kind of victorious reliquary for the destroyed body of Christ.

This vast place also has a 'holy emptiness" but it is in a place where the indigenous populations for millenia have had physical representations of gods or God or saints. It is especially strange that this latin American place has no iconic presences.

Santa Maria degli Angeli, Ticino, Switzerland and the Evry Cathedral

Mario Botta (Heathcote and Spens, Church Builders, pp. 138-147 and Dupre, Churches, pp. 8-17) has been commissioned to do some rather prestigious churches. The Cathedral at Evry in France is a spectacular twelve-story round building within a massive complex of red brick buildings, gardens and trees. The round cathedral, itself, is topped with a "crown" of lime trees. It has, however, its sanctuary at one end of the vast space, with black marble floor and white marble altar and black cross with white corpus above the center of the sanctuary. The sanctuary is quite dramatic. The sky comes in through the open glass ceiling.

There is a focal tree of life in an abstract black and white, immense terme window. The colors and materials are beautiful and typical of the materials used since Roman imperial times. But the church is not fit for anything but ritual prayer. There is no focus which would say come and sit.

The little chapel on a mountain top in his native Swiss city, Santa Maria degli Angeli also has reverberant imagery. The construction of a bridge with a vast arc of brick is reminiscent of the aqueducts of old. The fenestration both on the approach bridge and on the round wall of the chapel itself make allusion to the little windows of Roman and Byzantine brick structures all over Europe. The whole makes a stark presentation of a building within nature and against the elements. Externally the church is a monument to the modern mind in a natural body.

The black ceiling within is most dramatic against the concrete and warm woods but the arrangement of the seating is basically, again, long with the sanctuary at one end of the round chamber. The pews do line up alongside the sanctuary but they continue to face front. The image on the ceiling and into the silo-lighted image of hands conforms to the description of Botta's imagery with respect to the Virgin's place in salvation history. His description in Dupre's Churches (pp. 10 f) reads like the Litany of the Blessed Virgin Mary.

> The Cedar is Mary, because as the cedar puts down roots deep enough to enable it to grow higher than any other tree, so she was so deeply confirmed in humility as to allow her to soar above all others when she conceived her divine son…..The Olive, tree of peace, is Mary, whose twig carried by the dove to the ark marked the reconciliation of man and God….The Shadow…. The Sea… The Book… The Pomegranate…. The Rose… The Moon…etc.

The twenty-two embossed window paintings by Enzo Cucchi under the guidance of Fr. Giovanni Pozzi, are reminiscent of le Corbusier's drawings on the doors of the Notre Dame du Ronchamp or the Matisse drawings in the Chapelle du Rosaire in Vence. The whole has a theatrical presence. I am sure that any of these places works well in the appropriate hands of a competent presider but the images are quite "intellectual," hardly capable of commanding the response to the divine "orge" which Otto and van der Leeuw have found so necessary in the imagery of the mysterium tremendum et fascinans.

The "problem" of church design is given plenty of evidence in this one architect. Of obvious religious intent and creative inventiveness, he does not quite grasp the human need for devotional foci. His buildings are focused for ritual liturgy or for learning from performance or sermon, it is true, but they have no iconic presence for meditation. It would not matter really if the building were locked unless being used for liturgy or performance because, although it is beautiful, it is empty of the Presence. Like a beautiful museum without art in it or a comfortable theater without a production, the place has no utility except in liturgy or learning.

Beyond that, the "problem" articulated for Church and architects alike by the Vatican Council II was to look to design a church which would take the congregation, the People of God, seriously. If they are relegated to audience, again, as they were for the five hundred years of the Tridentine Liturgy, then the Vatican Council might as well not have made any study or declarations about the Liturgy.

The Church of the Year 2000

Perhaps we can see in the competition run by the Vatican for a church to commemorate the Jubilee some reasoning behind the present direction of church architecture. At least, we might ascertain some reasons why what is so, is so.

The list of architects who submitted designs or plans to the committee reads like a Who's Who of Pritzker Prize winners! These were asked: Richard Meier, Gunter Behnisch, Tadao Ando, Santiago Calatrava, Frank Gehry, and Peter Eisenman. Heathcote and Spens (Church Builders, pp. 208-219) supply drawings and commentary on much of the competition. Richard Meier's submission won the competition.

Each of the designs included a long plan with pews facing a blank wall behind a central altar. The exteriors were fabulous contrivances. The natural lighting for each of the liturgical spaces was to be indirect and subtle. The walls were all to be white.

The interesting fact is that none of the designs had much concern for the placing of the pulpit or for the presidential seat. The fact is the design has modern walls and modern lighting. There is provision for modern acoustics. There is, however no provision for organ or other musical accompaniment. Simply put there is little attention to anything that might pertain to the functioning of the spaces for the liturgy itself. The designs would all be stunning pieces of advertisement from the street view but have little or no advance on the catacomb or tomb chapels in the local Roman neighborhoods. This is rather a sad commentary.

Archbishop Weakland in his Commonweal article (op. cit., pp. 10 f) states that there is a problem in the restorationists' approach to the liturgy and the church. He looks to a book-length interview with Cardinal Ratzinger for some understanding of how the liturgy is to be "restored."

> The cardinal does not like the word "restoration" and yet his own words seem to justify the term as a label for this new development. He responds to Messori's question on whether a restoration is no motion in the church by saying: "If by 'restoration' is meant a turning back, no restoration of such a kind is possible.... But if by restoration we understand the search for a new balance after the exaggerations of an indiscriminate opening to the world, after the overly positive interpretations of an agnostic and atheistic world, well, then a restoration understood in this sense (a newly

> found balance of orientations and values within the Catholic totality) is altogether desirable and, for that matter, is already in operation in the church. In this sense it can be said that the first phase after Vatican II has come to a close." (Vittorio Messori, The Ratzinger Report, Ignatius Press, 1985)

So, when Weakland informs us that the word for the "sanctuary" in the documents about liturgy coming from the Vatican these days has been changed to "presbyterium," we have a clear idea that the place of the clergy is being secured in this new movement. At least, that is what Archbishop Weakland thinks. The change of a word like this one does have a certain significance. Perhaps, this is something to consider.

Chapter Nine: Fine Finish for Furnishings

Cathedra, Throne, Seat

The stone bench in the Catacomb of Priscilla attests to the early appreciation of the place of the presider. In fact for the first thousand years the congregation always stood. Visiting the imperial cathedrals of Russia, even today, the pilgrim/tourist is surprised to note the baldachin, often in rich cloth, over the place where the emperor and empress would attend the liturgy, apparently standing for the whole of their time in the church.

So, there are many examples of thrones or stone seats for patriarchal saints, like Augustine of Canterbury or Denis of Paris. There also developed the tradition of the fall stool for the visiting prelates of the Middle Ages who might preside at canonical chapters, monkish chapters, or public liturgies.

In the later periods, thrones were kept in cathedrals, representing the seat of the bishop. The chair for the priest is not the same thing. One will notice a mere priest sitting on one of those thrones probably never! The presider's chair is, therefore, a thoroughly modern invention. The priest sits for the readings only recently, after Vatican II.

The modernization of our understanding of the Lord's democratic availability and subjection to the laws of mankind, "...becoming obedient even to death, death on a cross...." has some vast significance. In the period after Vatican II, the sitting of even the priest amounts to a kind of comfort in the house of the Lord which is thoroughly "modern." Is it because of the influence of Buddhism in our trying to deal with other religions open-mindedly? Does it have something to do with learning that "Islam " means "acceptance" ? Is it because our understanding of how other great spiritual leaders were without crippling pride that we realize how humble was the Lord? Is this why our own churches put such emphasis on our equality with God —that He emphasized His equality with us? Does it, also perhaps, have something to do with the democratization dispensed by the literature of Marx and Engels' Socialism? "...From each according to ability, to each according to need..."?

Jesus entered into human life, incarnate God, to suffer with us, to help us to love the widow and orphan. He taught us to raise all our brothers and sisters to a level of equality with us. Interesting things to think about, yes, but the presence of that seat for the presider has a paradigmatic meaning that is new. We should consider whence we have come, where we are, and whither we go with this, precisely because, at this time, we have some say about who we will become.

Ambo, Pulpit, Lectern, Throne of the Book

In the early Church, as we have seen, the scriptures would have been read from a portable lectern or from a bema, usually a stone table for the purpose of reading , the custom taken directly from Hebrew liturgical practice.

The Romanesque and Gothic periods saw the development of monastic communities and canonical communities who prayed the liturgical hours in choir. This "choir," takes its name from Greek drama where a group called the "chorus" was employed to comment on the events of the play being ritually performed. The choir as a place was fitted with seats so that, when the group was not speaking, reading, or singing the prayer, they might sit. There is a bench at Torcello and at Saint Apollinaris in Classe which goes around the apsidal east end of the basilica. This is an early example of pre-Gothic choral arrangements.

During the fourth century a schola cantorum was begun in Rome. The development of choirs to sing developed as a connected school to the large liturgical centers. The place in the church for the singers eventually was cordoned off. It became a cancelleria by the height of the Middle Ages. Choir lofts would become raised balconies. In fact, among the most famous are those of Della Robbia and Donatello which were replaced in the Cathedral of Florence, on the occasion of a Medici marriage, because the scion of the family wanted a more "modern" wooden face on the singers' platform for his daughter's big day.

The cordoned-off choir for the monks or canons actually became enclosed rooms in the larger monastery or cathedral churches. The seats developed into individual stalls and eventually into rather elaborate throne-like mini-chambers with folding seats which could support a standing (slumping) monk on its misericorde, the shelf which protrudes from the bottom of the upraised seat in the individual stall. The choir was arranged around a large lectionery or book stand which would hold an immense prayer book with the chant in very bold print to be read, followed, sung, by all who could see it. This accounts for those immense illuminated manuscripts of chant and scripture, like the Lindisfarne Gospels and the Book of Kells.

After the rise of the mendicant preaching orders, the Franciscans and Dominicans, in the thirteenth century, preaching became much more important and the development of the pulpit ensued. The lectern was housed in a balcony or even an independent raised preaching aedicule. The sounding board behind or above developed as a baldachin which could project the voice over the crowds better than the apsidal end of the chancel. To better appeal to a larger crowd, the pulpit was moved to the middle of the nave, eventually becoming the place of an independent source of Renaissance entertainment. The sermon developed into a major form of civil coercion. The eucharist, at that time, had degenerated in public participation; it was something which the people might attend, might watch for the "showing" of the sacred species, but in which they would not participate directly. The altar facing the wall, the priest's back to them, the word read in Latin, made the pulpit and the organ much more important parts of the public worship of the Late Medieval and Renaissance Church.

Altar, Mensa, Tomb, Sarcophagus, Deus ex Machina,
Table, Treasure Chest

The functioning furniture of the church has had different forms throughout the history of the liturgy. The altar, for instance, has had many different forms whereby its form followed its function or was a symbol or metaphor for a function which it performs along with its use as a table, mensa. At one time, in the very beginning of the Christian era, the table was merely a thing on which the bread and wine were placed. Because of its use in the liturgies which united the living with the dead, the Church Suffering, Church Militant, and Church Triumphant in prayerful interaction, one praying to another for a third, it soon became a reliquary. Jungmann tells us that things used by the dead would be placed on the table to remember them and that eventually even body parts were placed there.

In order to regularize this practice, the altar became more recognizably a reliquary. There were compartments and eventually an altar stone with relics imbedded.

For the first five hundred years there would be only one altar in the church building according to Jungmann (Public Worship, pg. 61). After the development of Benedictine monasticism there were, at first, altars added to the rood screen and, later, on the walls of the nave, and then in ambulatories, eventually in a ring of altars surrounding the east end of the chancel of great churches. The chevet of the great Gothic cathedrals becomes a stunningly intricate corona of chapels with their flying buttresses, surrounding the main sanctuary of the east ends of Notre Dame de Paris,d'Amiens, de Reims, de Rouen, St. Vitus in Prague, Notre Dame in Strassbourg, Köln Cathedral, Léon Cathedral.

The altar had as its predecessor altar, the altars of Herod's or Solomon's Temple which had horns at the four corners. This altar image spoke of sacrifice. Christ is in the Eucharist, the "unbloody sacrifice;" this kind of altar reinforced His ultimate sacrifice on the cross. The literature spoke of the "oblation" and "immolation" of the victim in the Mass. Sometimes, the early altars seemed to resemble such an Old Testament altar.

It also appeared as a coffin or sarcophagus, often with the body of a dead saint, either miraculously preserved (as are Sts. Gervase and Protase, as well as St. Ambrose in Sant' Ambrogio in Milano, St. Catherine of Siena in Santa Maria Sopre Minerva in Rome, St. Lucy in Venice, St. Clare in Assisi, or St. Francis Xavier Cabrini in Fort Tryon, New York City).

There were also statues of bodies in similar sarcophagi like St. Francis Xavier in San Javier del Bac on the Tohono-O'Odham Reservation outside Tucson. That statue could do double duty as the Christ for Good Friday with its arms raised, or for Holy Saturday with its arms down, or for Easter with its whole being radiantly dressed and standing. This kind of thing comes during the traditions of the Middle Ages when figures were used for miracle and mystery plays as well as for celebratory processions.

Another predecessor would be the altar at the center of the Dionysiac rites in the amphitheaters of Greece and Rome. Archaeologists tell us that the proscenium arch and the skene, the backdrop, of the Renaissance, Baroque, and Greek Revivial, became the retablo or raredos, the backdrop to the altar, itself. There were two doors on either side of the mensa and a little opening or aedicule above it for the cross or the monstrance, a kind of deus ex machina, God appearing through a mechanical devise (from the ancient theater). In the Romanesque, Gothic, and Renaissance altars with such walls of sculpture and/or paint and the monstrance or cross under a baldachino, the whole program would speak of the eternal nature of the Christ in constant contact with both us and the heavenly court. In the Renaissance, this backdrop developed into what was called a sacra conversatione, a sacred dialogue, wherein the saints would converse with one another in a space/time reality that united them in full dress with one another as the Church Triumphant. The polyptychs of Giovanni Bellini, Tintoretto, Tiziano, Gaulli, Michelangelo. Raphael, Tilman Riemenschneider, Peter Paul Rubens, Murillo, Rublev, Paolo Veronese, Giotto di Bondone, Duccio di Buoninsegna, Simone Martine, Piero della Francesca, Mantegna, Velasquez, El Greco, Gerard David, Rogier van der Weyden, the Van Eycks, Petrus Christus, Michael Pacher, Albrecht Durer, Matthias Grunewald, all of these and thousands more became the thing for the faithful to concentrate on while the Mass faced the wall…..

Vatican II turned the altar around. With the restoration of the idea of the eucharist as meal, it became a table, a mensa, once again, looking like a table with legs and space. The need for the altar stone was suppressed. The Christ became more tangible, less awesome, more God-among-us. The documents recommended that the backdrop of the sacred ritual be not the raredos of theatrical and artistic production but the living Body of Christ, the people whom the congregants must love as themselves, according to the commandments given by Jesus.

A primary experience of the paradigmatic meaning of the altar

On a recent visit to Notre Dame de Paris there was a new arrangement in the crossing sanctuary for us to observe. I must confess that I have mulled over two visits for many years because it seemed that the meaning of Church had shifted between the visits and the shift was not comfortable. Just after Vatican II on the previous visit we noticed a lovely simplicity in the sanctuary. There was a large wooden refectory table with a single large candle and a single bouquet of flowers, a Louis XV arm chair as the presider's seat with a couple of backless Louis XVI stools for the other functionaries on either side of it in the sanctuary, a single pulpit on the plinth floor, level with the altar, with a lectern above at the entrance to and level with the traditional choir which begins at the east end of the crossing. The priests were few, one white-haired presiding with great dignity and warmth, the other dark-haired commenting from the lectern outside the sanctuary, welcoming, describing, translating for the congregation of foreign visitors. There was only one statue (the ancient sibilant Vierge de Notre Dame de Paris) on the southeast pier. The sun was pouring through the great south rose. The music was powerful but seeming to come from the background, filling the faithful from the shadows, like memories coming from the past. The whole experience was engaging and fulfilling, reverent toward God, yet respectful of the people.

It all seemed so right, then, whereas, the second time, it all seemed so wrong.

This time there were a couple of sets of candles. One large round table for votives, strewn all about with flowers, was to one side. There were other candles near the altar, and other flowers in front and in other places on the floor. There was an array of chairs of the Louis XIV variety (but having different legs) strewn purposelessly about, more than were needed for the Mass in progress. The altar, itself, was not a table but a large bronze-figured cube. The figures were elegant but faceless. They seemed to match the faceless figures now added to the northeast pier—in competition with the eleventh century Vierge de Paris sculpture on the southeast pier.

The problem with the altar was given flesh by the way in which the liturgy was conducted. There seemed to be so many sanctuary staff who were not really attentive to the congregation. The congregation seemed to be infiltrated by many milling tourists. The order of the Mass went on without much of a sense that the clergy had any converse with the people. The eucharistic procession was rather orderly but without music; there were a number of communion stations but the reception of the eucharist seemed to be pro forma and without more than the merest contact between ministers and communicants. The whole seemed efficient and heartless, ex opere operato, efficacious sacrament by reason of having been performed.

And so the altar which seemed like a treasure chest or oversized jewelry box is now not an altar of sacrifice, nor a table for the banquet, nor a tomb-reliquary for the holy predecessors, nor a base for the enthronement of the Eucharistic Presence. Neither is it a temporary table on which to place the offerings which are transformed into the Body and Blood of Christ. But it seems to be a safe in which is preserved some cultural heritage, or some political hegemony, secure from the vagaries of any congregation which might approach the liminal edge of the holy-of-holies where the electi, the members of the clerical cast for this liturgical drama, might touch them without meeting them.

The new paradigm is a strong box . The Church protected from the people. This may seem overstated but the clarity of my own experience leads me to worry about how the Church is handling disagreement. Remember Archbishop Weakland's note that the "restorationists" have changed the name of the "sanctuary" to the "presbyterium," the "place of the priests." (op. cit., pg. 10)

Suppression of the voice of the opposition is tantamount to closure of the treasury. Those who control the deposit of the Faith have no reason to consort with those who would participate in Christ's Church because those "un-initiates" might contaminate the treasure. This is not a comfortable state of affairs.

Where the Blame Might Land

Perhaps the furnishings of the churches are saying something about the state of the Church which must be listened to. Rudoplh Arnheim reflects on the reason for attending to doing the best one can:

> It has sometimes been argued that an architect's conception need be no more exacting than that of the average inhabitant, and that there is no good reason for providing what will not be noticed. Bu I shall have occasion to observe that the awareness comes at many different levels, not all explicitly conscious, and also that in any profession, as a matter of ethics and self-respect, the most intelligent vision must prevail, irrespective of how full it will be appreciated by clients, customers, or consumers. (Dynamics of

Architectural Form, pg. 101)

Since the arts are mostly silenced, this "clash of uncoordinated orders" speaks volumes. Arnheim coins this phrase (ibid., pg. 171) in considered response to Robert Venturi's insight that the aesthetic of American building today is "inherent contradiction" (ibid., pg. 163).

Arnheim also realized that

> In religious architecture, caprice has been offered almost unlimited liberty and eagerness to attract a dwindling clientele at almost any cost is expressed externally in ostentatious shape and color. Inevitably churches have taken their cues from their leading competitors, the entertainment and catering industries and their barbarous imagery. Such willingness to sacrifice the end to highly dubious means is possible only because the very nature of religion and its tasks are now so open to question that their external expression is no longer governed by reliable standards. These tendencies make all the more rewarding those examples of church architecture that succeed in translating dignity and spiritual devotion into twentieth-century idioms.(ibid., pg. 206).

He states further that a "successful church" is a "statement of spiritual aspirations" (ibid., pg. 216). So what can we glean from the experience of Notre Dame in Paris, once as a wonderful place and then as a horrible place to experience liturgy? Well what are the differences in spiritual aspirations that make it once a "successful church" and then an unsuccessful one?

Perhaps, the most significant difference is in the way the congregation was treated. The welcome and reverence at the former visit made a tremendous impact on the experience of being included in the ritual prayer. The lighting also made a big difference. One cannot command the sun to shine through the south rose whenever there is a liturgy. The attention to detail, however, made an impression. "Attention to detail" is, after all, what John Dewey describes in Art as Experience as the essential element which makes a work into an artwork. Mies' second most famous phrase: "God is in the details," fits into this discussion as well.

The lack of attention to detail from the under-interested "professionals" in the Church, whether they be concerned with the environment, the music, or the ritual itself, can, if they do little enough of their job, make a great deal of intrusion into the experience of the people of God. Those who do not do enough can get in the way of the experience. It is necessary to recognize that fact. Because, no matter how well done the church or the artistic environment in the decorated domus, the addition of careless confusion can confound the word of the Lord, the work of the Spirit, and diminish "the greater glory of God."

Chapter Ten: Architectural Motivations

Architectural Motivations

There are quite a few periods of architecture that we have considered and quite a vast number of aesthetic traditions; we need look at examples of historical edifices to experience their environments. We want to understand how the immutable liturgy takes place within different cultures, to consider just what it is that is "immutable."

The Early Christian Era affords us precious few, if any, examples of places that were used when they simply commemorated the sacred meal of the Last Supper. The byzantine imperial tradition gives us a few more but these are larger and more specifically set places for the rites of religion, baptism and eucharist, principal among them. The correlation and commemoration of the "Church Suffering," the "Church Militant," and the "Church Triumphant," in church buildings, had an eventual effect in the buildings' dedication to especially holy people. Their hierophanies led to the saving and reverencing of things touched by them as sources of holy or even godly power, or kratophanies. The churches became reliquaries. People sought to access the kratos, the power, through pilgrimage.

The Romanesque Era is full of differing kinds of building, constructed over a thousand years and covering most of Europe. These grow bigger and more grand, changing from fortress to house of pilgrimage with what appears to us as little change in decorative motif. The Gothic developments after the crusades present us with masterpieces of glass and ever expanding forests of stone from the introduction of the pointed arch and the flying buttress in the eleventh century right up to the present with the unfinished Cathedral of St. John the Divine in NYC and the Sagrada Familia in Barcelona. The pilgrimage place turned into castle. Then there's the Renaissance, the Baroque, the Rococco, the Neo Classical, the revivals, Arts and Crafts, Art Nouveau, Moderne, and Deco, the Bauhaus, and

Post Modern movements with all their variations on architectural themes.

Do we need to visit all the churches? Do we need examples of each style? Indeed, does the naming of a "style" actually mean that there are interrelated elements which make these periods of art history discretely distinct? Does that matter in our consideration of what is immutably necessary in the churches we intend to build for the future?

These significant questions become irrelevant against the certain backdrop. Do we have such a "certain backdrop"?

The Certain Backdrop

If I may, I would like to take a stab at what it is that is essential. On the one hand the building has functions. In the past those functions included the great baptismal rite, the penitential rituals, place for miracle and mystery plays, parades, sleeping pilgrims, those seeking sanctuary, monks, nuns, canons all seated in misericordes and choir stalls, vast audiences attentive to lectures, sermons, organ recitals.

There have been innumerable "functions" housed within church buildings. Different eras had different needs. But there are presently some needs that church buildings serve in our own day. What are they? Does their accommodation demand totally different buildings than those that have gone before? Is adaptation advisable or attainable?

There are times when communities need large spaces for worship and other times when they need smaller spaces simply because of the size of the congregation or their focus. Should there be different buildings or can the same building fit all needs?

Let us narrow our quest. Consider that a church building must immediately seem appropriate for the essential meeting with God. That is a primordially necessary function as we have discovered it. Then consider the functions that have to be afforded primary permanence in the church building in order to insure that this "meeting" not be hindered. This is where we must think of the purposes of the building. It seems that there are three general realms of purpose which arise from those myriad functions enumerated above from the history of church building.

Primary Functions

A church is used for ritual worship, This includes the Mass or Eucharistic Liturgy itself, wherein the congregation, united with the whole Church throughout time and space, re-enacts the Christ sacrifice and commemorative meal in considering His birth, death, and resurrection. This is the prime function of Catholic churches. It has been their prime function since liturgical time began, although, as we have seen, it sometimes took second or third place to some far less important ritual or theatrical enterprise.

It also developed quite early that the story needed to be told and so the churches became places for learning. This includes listening to sermons and homilies. But it grew to include looking at pictures on canvas, stone, and glass. Then, too, listening to communal prayers, recited, sung, and/or performed became a way to learn about the Lord and the consequences of His mystery. So the churches became places of audience. The NAVE, the place for the congregation in a church, calls forth the image of the church as a ship. The metaphor suggests that the large space full of the people of God is afloat on the sea of life; the captain bringing the passengers and crew home to safe harbor. The church building has sometimes even been made to look like a ship. The larger the nave the more need the people seem to have for a leader, a commander, a shepherd.

There also developed a sense of the church on the landscape as the place where the individual could find "safe harbor." The church became a place for the individual to come to practice devotion, to meditate, to seek and find the encounter with "the holy." The church then becomes a place for contemplation, private contemplation, at that.

Secondary Functions (supporting the primary)

These three functions of the church building: ritual, learning, and contemplation, have been the reasons behind much of the history of church architecture. Sometimes the buildings were grand, even grandiose, sometimes, most intimate, even personal places. The accoutrements of the places, however, have developed, according to Eliade and his disciples, along the same lines across religions and cultures. It stands up to scrutiny, therefore, for us to consider just what are the things that have become necessary in our history for the proper set-up of churches.

The use of art to build beautiful places is, apparently, one of those intangible characters constituent of our very humanity. Only we do this: make our environment over according to our taste. Chimpanzees don't, parrots don't, dolphins don't do this; we do. We decorate our world.

Jean Auguste Dominique Ingres, one of the most famous of the presidents of the French Academy, insisted that taste is a matter of education.

> There are not two arts, there is only one: it is the one which has as its foundation the beautiful, which is eternal and natural. Those who seek elsewhere deceive themselves, and in the most fatal manner. ("Art and the Beautiful," Artists on Art from the XIV to the XX Century, ed. Robert Goldwater and Marco Treves, Pantheon 1945, 1972, pg. 216)
>
> It is rarely other than the lower type of the arts, whether in painting or in poetry or in music, which naturally pleases the multitude. The more sublime efforts of art have no effect at all upon uncultivated minds. Fine and delicate taste is the fruit of education and experience. All that we receive at birth is the faculty of creating such taste in ourselves and for cultivating it, just as we were born with a disposition for receiving the laws of society and for conforming to their usages. It is up to this point, and no further, that one may say that taste is natural to us. ("Taste," ibid. pg. 216)

So, rather than the hegemony of mere preference, TASTE is the result of learning how to make or perceive "the beautiful." In this Ingres seems to agree with Pythagoras, Vitruvius, Fibonacci, da Vinci, and le Corbusier. Seeing proportion as an intrinsic beauty in nature, recognized by humans and forever sought in making over the world.

In our own era taste has slipped into the background. Herbert Muschamp, architecture critic of the New York Times says,

> Architects operate in an increasingly competitive market and in an

> aesthetically eclectic period that is not guided by educated consensus on matters of taste or style. The profession benefits from the myth that its members cannot be qualitatively ranked. ("Arts and Leisure," Sunday, December 30, 2001, pg 36)

To the question "How can you criticize people for doing what they think is right?" Muschamp's "…routine answer: 'I read a lot of history.'," is a reinforcement of the pursuit in which we are now engaged, is it not?

In our consideration of the things necessary for church buildings, we will look at things of beauty, BUT we are not interested in these forms as things of beauty per se but rather we seek to understand how the form serves the function. The primary function of a church being to encourage the encounter with the MYSTERY, we must consider not whether the churches are beautiful but whether or not they serve their function beautifully. This is the "educated taste" befitting the intelligent Catholic.

This becomes primarily a quest for architectural excellence then, does it not? We are looking to see how the church can make the people of God ready for the encounter in ritual, learning, and contemplation. So the beauty lies in the way the parts come together in the building, not the way the parts stand on their own. The church, as a "unity of coordinated orders" would, thus, be a microcosmic universe in which we seek the experience of the macrocosmic, of the Totally Other, Eliade's "Ganz Andere," the triune God.

A Disclaimer

We do not wish to say that beauty does not count. We especially do not want to say that there is no place for beauty. Indeed, with all my heart, I believe that we should put beauty at the service of faith whenever, wherever, however we can. But to consider what is most beautiful in a church building is to miss the point of this essay. We are trying to see what is essential. Beauty may indeed be necessary for those with educated taste but the question must remain: What of beauty is essential?

In fact, Otto speaks early of the orge experience of the majestas tremenda which "clothes itself in symbolical expressions—vitality, passion, emotional temper, will, force, movement, excitement, activity, impetus," (Idea of the Holy pg. 23), the same elemental expressions which Eliade attributes to a kratophany. (Myths, Dreams, and Mysteries, trans. Philip Mairet, Harper & Row, 1975, pg. 126).

Van der Leeuw says we are speaking about, "...the awe-inspiring divine orge, that about the holy which excites fear...a nuance of the awe-inspiring...the ghostly, the ghastly..." Further he says, "We become still closer to the holy through the influence of darkness and semi-darkness...through the impenetrable darkness is indicated the fact that the deity 'dwells in unapproachable light.'" (Sacred and Profane Beauty, pp 190-192)

Ugliness seems to become necessary in making things that encourage encounter with God. He talks of ugly virgin statues as somehow affording a better entrée for the imagination and therefore an easier access to the contemplative consideration of the mystery behind the artwork. We might consider the Virgen del Pilar in Saragossa Spain, or the big-headed Christ of Monreale in Sicily. The Avignon Pieta in the Louvre brings up very deep feelings of grief to many of its viewers. The unfinished last Pieta of Michelangelo in the Museo del Duomo in Florence, Italy also affords a great entering into the mystery of the death of Christ. The Isenheim Altarpiece, the Rublev Trinity, the Vladimir Madonna, the Black Virgin of Montserrat, all of these images tell of the rightfulness of Otto's, Eliade's, and van der Leeuw's suggestion: a certain human ugliness in an aesthetically beautiful product can engage the encountering spirit in a way that puts that spirit at ease and allows the mystical encounter to proceed beyond the encounter with the beautiful object.

Van der Leeuw puts further flesh on the idea:

> ...when God needs a house he lays claim to everything. There beauty may serve, but not rule. We are not thinking of the ugliness of carelessness...We are not thinking of a negation, but of a positive demand. In God's house God must reign; his thoughts must find expression in the building, and if men are not otherwise able to understand them, they must be expressed at the expense of beauty. Here lie the preconditions for a conflict. (ibid. pg. 202)

However, again, we are not about to consider the ugliness of things in this approach to the appropriateness of the church space. Things may be beautiful or not. They may encourage the encounter or not; this is a critical question but not the critical consideration! What we are looking for is the essential elements that make a space seem right for those three functions: ritual, learning, and contemplation, against the "prime directive," build God a house—a place that encourages the encounter with the myserium tremendum et fascinans. God's house must invite us to engage the OTHER who both attracts and repels us in our ritual, learning, and contemplation.

Conclusion

So, where are we? It seems that we are building lots of long planned churches in a period after an ecumenical council. The Vatican Council II documents seemed to many to suggest that a church-in-the-round better fit the ecclesiology and theology. However, we have very few buildings that surround the sanctuary with the Body of Christ. What does that say? Are we defiant? Or does the voice of the faithful simply reject that recommendation? St. Augustine did point out that there are three arms of the mind of the Church, the theologians, the magisterium, and the sensus fidelium (the intellectuals, the hierarchy, the rank-and-file faithful)

Another reality is that very few of the newest church buildings give any space for the visual representation of the stories of Christendom. It even seems quite profoundly that "lesser" forms of devotion like the rosary, the stations, lighting candles, are frowned upon. Without statues, where do those devotional motivations land? Is this the "better taste" of the Church leadership at work? Or is it simply a concurrence with the agnostic or atheistic intellectualism of our world? Or less, is it a response to the commercial anthropocentrism of our day?

The fact is that we have precious little sacred space, even though we are covering the suburban landscape with mall churches, places which put God among us. Is this profoundly real and good for a peasant class of rich bourgeoisie?

Or should we be examining ourselves a little more deeply and finding a need to seek God with less conviction and more fear than we have allowed ourselves lately?